CLEAR MIND
OPEN HEART

CLEAR MIND
OPEN HEART

HEALING YOURSELF,
YOUR RELATIONSHIPS,
AND THE PLANET

EDDIE AND DEBBIE SHAPIRO

THE CROSSING PRESS
FREEDOM, CALIFORNIA

Copyright © 1998 by Eddie and Debbie Shapiro
Cover design by Tara M. Eoff
Cover photograph by S. Autrum-Mulzer with permission
  from Staatliches Museum Für Völkerkunde
Printed in the U.S.A.

First published in 1994 by Judy Pitakus (Publishers) Ltd.

For information on bulk purchases or group discounts for this and other Crossing Press titles, please contact our Special Sales Manager at 800-777-1048 x214.

Visit our Web site on the Internet: www.crossingpress.com

Library of Congress Cataloging-in-Publication Data

Shapiro, Eddie. 1942-
    Clear mind, open heart: healing yourself, your relationships, and the
planet / by Eddie & Debbie Shapiro.
        p. cm.
    Rev. ed. of: A time for healing. 1994.
    Includes bibliographical references and index.
    ISBN 0-89594-917-2 (pbk.)
    1. Spiritual healing. I. Shapiro, Debbie, 1953-. II. Shapiro, Eddie,
1942- Time for healing. III. Title.
  BL65.M4S46   1998
    158–dc21   98-10690
                                                                        CIP

Contents

To Bill and Sheila Feeney
and to Chrysalis

We would particularly like to thank Gill Cormode and Anne Lawrance for their great editing; Philip Cotterell for his good spirit; Susan Mears, our super–special agent and her husband Jonathan; Fiona Fredenburgh and Dr. Bernie Siegel.

Special thanks for the generosity of those people who contributed their personal stories to this book. We also want to thank our family and friends for their kind support.

Introduction

This book is our offering to all fellow travellers who want to heal their lives, to bring sanity and goodness to our shared existence, and to wake up to the peace and freedom that is within each one of us. We are in this world for such a short time; life is so precious, a gift to be enjoyed. It is a great blessing. Each one of us is important – no one is insignificant.

The healing journey is the journey of a lifetime; it is an awakening of the heart. This involves a deep commitment to oneself and a desire to find real meaning in life. We, the authors, are both journeyers, having been involved with our own spiritual path for many years. Along the way we have been with luminous and inspiring teachers. They have given us strength in moments of weakness, doubt and confusion, and have guided us with their love and wisdom.

We were married in London and then went to India for our honeymoon. It is a diverse and fascinating country, full of ambiguity and vibrancy. We thought it would be an opportunity to explore the mystical and spiritual wealth India is known for. We spent time with the teachers we had trained with and we were also fortunate to have a personal audience with and receive teachings from the Dalai Lama.

We had arrived in Dharmsala, northern India, where the Dalai Lama has his palace, only to be told that he was in Rome. A few days previously there had been a meeting in Assisi between the Pope, the Dalai Lama, and many other religious leaders, such as the then Archbishop of Canterbury, Robert Runcie, the head of the Greek Orthodox Church and a representative of the Native Americans. It was the first meeting of its kind and therefore a historic occasion. Now it was three days later and we felt certain that the Dalai Lama would have returned to his palace. We were right, and our audience with him was confirmed.

The meeting was for just the three of us, sitting comfortably and discussing certain issues; at times he tightly held our hands. He told us how the meeting of the many religious leaders had been an important experience for everyone involved, as it was a real time for healing. He vividly described one morning when the delegates were walking towards the Vatican and nearby was a group of Jewish people. With tears running down their cheeks, they were crying out, 'Lama, Lama, shalom, shalom, peace, peace.' The Dalai Lama told us, 'I immediately broke protocol and ran across the street to chat with them!'

He explained how peace must start with each one of us, with every moment and in every action; that in healing ourselves by developing communication, forgiveness, loving-kindness and compassion, we can offer a helping hand to others.

Meetings with such influential and remarkable beings as the Dalai Lama have encouraged us to continue with our own journey. Along the way we have met others whose journeys have touched our heart and, we feel, will touch yours. The personal stories in this book have come from participants in our workshops, and from friends and peers who have entered into their own healing. They agreed to share their experiences as an inspiration to others. We have also included some of our own (marked with a vertical rule). What one person has done, all of us can do. Healing *is* possible, and it is needed now.

EDDIE AND DEBBIE SHAPIRO

1

HEALING
IS
WHOLENESS

*The beginning of the path of healing
is the end of life unlived*
STEPHEN LEVINE

Have you ever wondered what it would be like if the world was a peaceful place? A place with no wars or abuse, where people lived with respect, dignity and care for themselves and each other? A place where you and I would accept and delight in our differences? John Lennon asked if we could 'imagine all the people sharing all the world, with no need for greed or hunger'. In our hearts, do we want a better life for ourselves and our families? To live in a world with greater understanding and compassion?

If we do, then it appears we have few choices: continue as we are, hurting both ourselves and each other; know things need to change but not act on it; or begin to heal. Is it not time to enjoy this profound gift of life? Can we reconcile our grievances, resolve and release our conflicts?

The healing journey is one of discovery, taking us to the very heart of our being. We can begin this journey at any time, whether or not we are dealing with physical illness, psychological or emotional issues. For the healing is of our whole self, not just one particular part. It is meeting ourselves on every level to find that which is holding us back from living a full, caring and responsive life. To heal is to hear our lost voices, to rediscover our forgotten selves. It is a transformative process, taking us from who we have been to who we really are. Gently and tenderly we open the heart to discover the love that is there.

Healing asks that we recognize and let go of conditioned modes of behaviour, prejudices and preconceived thought patterns. This means accepting that which is keeping the heart from being open: the mistrust, fear, hurt or rejection. The parts of ourselves we have pushed away and tried to forget: the child who felt lonely or was punished, the lover who was spurned, times of anger, moments of guilt, mistakes made. It is a full acceptance of our human condition: the vulnerability and impermanence, the joys and the heartaches.

For there are so many wounds and atrocities that have taken place in the name of freedom, politics, religion, or through greed and selfishness. So much misunderstanding within ourselves and between families, friends, races and countries. And yet there is also a place inside each of us that does not want to keep hurting, a place that aches for mercy, healing and happiness.

I am stopping myself. I blame my husband, my circumstances. I blame my parents for the way they brought me up. I feel I have wasted so many years feeling hopeless and depressed. I want to understand myself desperately in order to be released from my physical and emotional pain.

SUSAN JOHNSTONE

Fundamentally, I am terrified. My mother died when I was seven years old and I believe I have to work through the pain of her death

2

before I can be happy. This leaves me even more scared and focused on a pain that I can't really feel. I often find myself very angry and irritable. The stress of holding this back and being nice in society is exhausting. I just want to be happy!

J.K.

We have gone to the moon and explored the vast reaches of outer space, yet we are only just beginning to understand ourselves and to explore the depths of our own being. We have yet to dive into the vast beauty that lies hidden, like a pearl in an oyster, waiting to be found. All the external satisfactions that could be wanted are at our fingertips, but the internal dissatisfactions continue, relationships break down, and to be peaceful or loving is rare. We go to religion and to therapy, to the teachers and the teachings, searching for answers. For no matter how far outwards we explore, beneath lies a longing for peace, a yearning to be home in the place where we know we belong.

Underlying the high life, the joys and the heartaches, was always an inner emptiness and a restlessness of soul which paced like a caged tiger in my depths.

MUZ MURRAY

This book is a call to all those who are sincere and ready to make the commitment to their journey, to come forth with a renewed spirit. It asks us to step into the unknown, to take chances and make changes, to come alive! It is a time to see through the limitations that bind us to old ways of thinking that have not worked and to connect with that which inspires and uplifts. It is an opportunity to be honest, to listen to our hearts and to open to a more tender and sensitive way of being. We do not have to get ill before we are healed – our healing is in every moment. We can make breakthroughs without needing to break down.

TO HEAL IS TO BECOME WHOLE

To understand the landscape that surrounds the journey to wholeness, it is necessary first to clarify our terms. In particular, as this book is involved with healing, it is important to differentiate between healing and curing.

To cure is to mend or bring something that is unwell to a state of wellness, and it is usually concerned with the particular part that is unwell, rather than with the whole. For instance, a broken bone can be cured by putting it in a cast, a disease can be cured by eliminating the diseased parts, and depression can be cured by taking an anti-depressant. The act of curing something should not be underestimated: that which is broken does need to be fixed, diseased parts often need to be removed, medicines do play a vital role in our sense of well-being.

Invariably, however, curing does not affect the larger issues involved, such as the original cause of the disease; eliminating the problem does not necessarily eliminate the cause. Therefore the cause may create further difficulties of a similar nature. Nor does curing deal with the side-effects of the disease on related parts – effects that can be very debilitating. As a dear friend of ours said, it was only after he was 'cured' of cancer that he became aware of how damaged was the rest of his being.

Healing is not directly involved with curing and it is not so concerned with individual parts. To heal means to become whole; it is to come into a wholeness of body, mind and heart. Healing can be seen as a gathering together of all the various parts of ourselves, even those seemingly unrelated parts and especially those that have become separate, ignored or denied. We bring all these into a conscious connectedness. In this sense, the healing journey is that of an awakening by ourselves to ourselves. It is the ultimate journey we can make, for it is a uniting of ourselves with who we really are.

Each of us has a story, each of us experiences conflict and hurt as we grow. This is the stuff we can work with and work through, in order to find our wholeness. In acknowledging ourselves we are stepping into the journey. It can seem like such a big step – where to begin, how to do it, what happens next? – but in the very moment that we are willing to see ourselves just as we are, when we bring our conscious awareness into action, it is in that moment that our healing begins.

During my school years I became further and further separated from my deepest inner self and everything that sustained me. I had no interest in boys or parties and had very few friends. The sixties passed me by completely! I was only dimly aware of names like the Beatles and the Rolling Stones. After school I spent a disastrous eighteen months in a religious order. My worst anguish was of a sense of utter worthlessness and hopelessness in the face of the overpowering mammoths of morality and religious obligation. Personal happiness, I was told, was of no importance. Eventually I had to leave as I had anorexia nervosa. I was wasting away. Never having seen myself in a mirror at the convent I was shocked, when I returned home, to see that I looked like a corpse. I felt an utter failure. A turning point came when I read about a young woman who had starved herself to death. Deep inside I knew then that I could also die. From that very moment I began to recover.

KARUNA KING

In his book *The Healing Path*, Marc Barasch describes five different aspects of the healing process. They are: Sensitization, Acceptance of Pain, Finding Meaning, Restoration of Balance, and Willingness to Change. Looking at these a little more closely, we see how Sensitization means a restoring of communication with the different parts of ourselves, a listening to our inner voice, and a sensitivity to what is happening in our body. Acceptance of Pain means a surrendering to and acceptance of what is happening, rather than a pushing away, denial or ignoring of our difficulties.

To Find Meaning is to discover for ourselves the deeper implications of our disease, the many ways we are learning and growing due to inner changes taking place. Restoration of Balance is to remember and reconnect with the healthy aspects of ourselves, so that any distress is seen in proportion to the whole and does not completely dominate. Willingness to Change means an openness to changing our thoughts and lifestyle patterns, so that we do not get stuck in ways that are not working towards our healing.

When we have a physical illness it is something tangible, and in most cases we have something visible to relate to. It may be difficult and restrictive, but it is right in front of us and we can work with what needs to be done. Psychological and emotional areas that need to be healed are not so specific or visible, yet they are just as important. They need a deeply honest and personal approach. This involves opening to that which has been emotionally closed, releasing that which has become psychologically painful, even numb, and reconnecting with ever deeper layers of personal understanding and insight.

All the different aspects of ourselves are intimately connected. A physical difficulty may therefore act as a stimulus for a psychological or emotional healing: as physical pain takes us deeper, it breaks through our normal sense of ourselves and throws us into a previously unknown space.

I understood that the illness and pain were great teachers for me. I recognised that in some way I needed to be rendered spineless and dependent. Day by day, almost hour by hour, I reflected upon what was happening and why. I spoke to the pain and to my wrecked body. I asked it to communicate to me in feelings, intuitions and images. In this way I came in touch with layer upon layer of psychological wounding and resentment and with the need to control. At the core of it all was fear, guilt and a compulsion to prove myself. I deliberately called all this stuff up into my consciousness. Sometimes with terrible imagery, sometimes with tears, sometimes very subtly, it all surfaced so that it could be healed and integrated. The illness was an acute taskmaster. But somewhere deep within me was a source of power and wisdom that knew I needed to go through such lessons. My psychological skin was too thick, my patterns so ingrained and unconscious, that only this painful spinelessness could touch me and force me to give attention to my real wounds. Nothing else could have stopped me in my tracks and given me the insights and healing.

WILLIAM BLOOM

6

Healing our lives means healing every part of ourselves. It is not about curing but about well-being, where we experience the whole picture, not just an isolated part. For some this may involve going on a spiritual quest, while for others it may mean spending more time with their families. Each of us finds his or her own path. One of the most healed people we know lives in a wheelchair. She gets on with raising her son, painting pictures and helping others. She has resolved her anger and resentment and found forgiveness. To heal is to bring compassion and awareness to that which we have rejected or withdrawn from; it is to bring acceptance and tenderness to all parts of our being.

EMBRACING PAIN AND SUFFERING

Due to being human and having a body, feelings, senses, dreams, desires, perceptions, thoughts and ideas, we are going to feel pain. There are the physical wounds as the body becomes entangled in the physical world; the emotional distress of experiencing broken love affairs or rejected feelings, loss or betrayal; and the psychological agony of failure or defeat, impermanence and change, of dreams unlived or unfulfilled. These experiences are not unique, but a natural part of being alive. There is pain, just as there is pleasure and joy. However, there is a tendency to forget that this pain is natural and either to hold on to the discomfort, or to try to push it away and deny it.

When we hold on to pain, we create more suffering. Through that suffering we may well believe we are redressing the balance, redeeming ourselves, or paying our dues for hurt that has been caused: 'How can I be happy if I have caused pain?' Our continued suffering somehow makes the guilt bearable. Mary had not been present at the death of her husband some four years previously. She believed that she needed to continue to suffer in order to assuage her guilt, that her suffering proved how she was a truly loving wife. This type of suffering is not a natural acceptance of life's conflicts, but a

7

clinging to the pain, and thus a continuation of it beyond its natural time.

I have needed to suffer to punish myself for my father's death. It has been a big part of me, I cannot give myself pleasure easily without having worked or suffered first. I am still suffering for believing I was a bad girl, not good enough. How can I be happy when I was never a good girl to my father?

DONNA SIMONS

Nor is a solution to be found in pushing away our feelings. That which we deny or ignore can build up and gather momentum, until we either burst out in a destructive explosion, or become numb not just to the ignored feelings, but to all our feelings. If we try to keep one thing repressed, we often find ourselves repressing everything.

We do not have to create more suffering, we do not have to add to the hurt that is already there, nor do we have to deny it. Pain need not dominate our lives or fill our every waking moment. Rather, it is telling us that something needs our attention. We can hold our pain gently, be with it, accept it, allow it a place in our lives. We can see if it has a purpose and become aware of how, through it, we are growing and reaching into ourselves with greater tolerance and compassion.

In the midst of terrible pain we can either find the event senseless or we can find sense in it. This is a conscious choice. There are no visible angels fluttering around saying, 'Hey! Enjoy the learning experience.' We need to choose to perceive and experience that pain has an inner logic and purpose. Is this a matter of blind faith? I think not. All aspects of our world seek to unfold to fulfil their potential. When we experience old forms, old attitudes, old ideas and patterns melting and transforming, it can be a painful affair. If we have wisdom we do not deny but accept the suffering — because the suffering has purpose. It is the friction that smooths us off, the disintegration and turmoil that integrates. It is often the source of great lessons about compassion and love. It is part of the total human process.

WILLIAM BLOOM

8

When we feel our own pain, we suffer; when we see the pain of the world we suffer. Seeing the starving, the homeless, the war orphans, the abused and the victims of injustice – this suffering fills our being and in the process it breaks through the walls around our heart. No longer can we be indifferent and uncaring. Compassion arises which softens and embraces. It acts as a catalyst to go further, for us to find more meaningful answers, to reach out to more people, to live with more love in our lives. The awareness of suffering brings alive the motivation to awaken, to understand, to care and to heal. As we talked with the Dalai Lama in India, he explained to us how, whenever there is a threat of war or devastation, the opposite arises: the urging for peace is awakened in the hearts of people everywhere.

My understanding is how I create my pain because I forget where peace is to be found. I forget where the answers to my difficulties lie. I externalise my problems so much that there is a split between my body and my mind and in time that split becomes painful. I know that bringing my mind back into my body releases the pain, but so often I do not allow the full process of healing to take place. There is too much pressure to be cured, to get better, so I do not take the time to honour what is happening. I can remove the symptoms and get rid of the pain, but that does not heal the pain. I know that my peace is in the present moment, that I do not have to wait until all the conditions are right, until I am perfect! My peace is here and now, whatever the circumstances. As I lie with my pain I know, really know, that I am not concerned about getting better. I just deeply want to become whole.

HELEN HUMPHRIES

DISCOVERING OUR PURPOSE

To sustain and nourish ourselves as we go on our journey we need to connect with purpose, with the real reason why we are doing all this in the first place. For, in many ways, to find meaning *is* to find healing. The word remission, which is normally used to mean the regression of disease, can also be

9

seen as meaning the refinding of our mission, our purpose, our true vocation. In reconnecting with our mission, we find our healing. Purpose stimulates motivation and perseverance. Without it we easily give up when the going gets rough, succumb to fear or slip back into old habits. It is the foundation from which the journey derives its momentum. As one-time US President Theodore Roosevelt so clearly said, 'Not once in a thousand times is it possible to achieve anything worth achieving except by labour, by effort, by serious purpose and by willingness to take risks.'

To connect with purpose means first looking at our basic thought patterns about why we are here and what life is meant to be about. For instance, most people agree that freedom is our birthright, but what that freedom means is interpreted differently by each culture. In most Western countries we think of it as the freedom of choice, such as to marry who we wish or live wherever we want; whereas others elsewhere in the world may think of freedom as simply being able to walk down a road without being stopped, or to read poetry in public. And while for some the meaning of life is reflected in the creativity and value of the possessions they are accumulating, for others it is seen in a single handful of rice, or perhaps the continuation of the family blood line. When we were travelling to London by train once, we got talking with the man sitting opposite us. As the conversation became more personal we began discussing the meaning of life. The man told us that, for him, 'Life is about procreating. I have my two children, so I've completed my purpose for being here.'

And yet, were we born only in order to procreate, to gain possessions, grow old and to die – and that's it? There is nothing wrong with having what we want or need, but perhaps, when we crave new things, we are not so much fulfilling the desire for something new as actually trying to fill an endless yearning, a deeper ache within. Maybe the longing is less for the object of desire as for a sense of completion and fulfilment of a different nature, of a spiritual and tender-hearted nature. The American visionary Edgar Cayce said, 'The ultimate purpose of our life is to rejoin God in conscious participation of divinity.' If we shift the object of our craving and begin to yearn for healing and peace more than anything else in our lives, then a deeper fulfilment does occur – an awareness that brings greater satisfaction and joy.

Do you think that such fulfilment could never be yours – that you do not deserve it, are too fixed in your ways to be able to embrace it, or that only the chosen few get it? We recently met a woman who has a life-threatening illness. She told us that she could never be at peace while she was ill – her mind was obsessed by her illness, her every waking moment was filled with fears and worries. She could not relax into herself for she was dominated by not feeling in control of what was happening to her physically. Fear would engulf her. Before she met us, she had not considered that it was possible and even helpful for her recovery and greater sense of well-being, that she spend time being quiet, relaxing and developing a peaceful attitude. By identifying with the illness she was making life more difficult; she was losing touch with who she was in herself and forgetting the rest of her being. Another woman told us how she could never be at peace until her daughter and her grandchildren were happy, and as her daughter was experiencing difficulties this was probably going to take some time!

Why is it that we put off our peace and happiness? What are our real priorities and values? Life is short, and we have a choice. We can watch ourselves getting older and becoming more resentful because life is slipping away and somehow we are not getting what we want out of it. Or we can stop and take a good look at our underlying attitudes and behaviour and how they influence our daily life. We can dream the years away or we can choose to wake up from the dream and put our inner yearnings into action.

I went to visit my father in a nursing home. He didn't even know my name. We went for a walk and he would just keep repeating 'I want to go to bed!' I looked around and saw so much sadness and confusion. I vowed then to work with myself – to try to be flexible in every situation, to meditate, relax, be physically active, to care about myself, to try not to take myself too seriously and to do lots of laughing!

EDDIE

11

Life will pass; no matter how hard we try to deny or stop it, we are impermanent beings. The facts of life – that we are born, we grow, we enjoy, we feel pain, we age and we die – are undeniable. What we do with these facts is the clue to our healing. For we can either sink into them and immerse ourselves in the cycle of wanting and getting and wanting and always being on the edge of dissatisfaction; or we can see through the impermanence of life and begin to understand more deeply, to enter into that which has real meaning and enduring joy. As Nadine Stair, an eighty-one-year-old woman from Kentucky, says in a poem: 'If I had my life to live over, I would start barefoot in the spring and stay that way later in the fall. I would go to more dances. I would ride more merry-go-rounds. I would pick more daisies.'

Engrossed in the ups and downs of life's distractions, we easily miss the beauty of each thing for what it is. John Lennon put it perfectly when he said, 'Life is what happens when you're busy making other plans.' We can be so focused on the past and what has happened, or on the future and what might happen, that the present is completely missed. After going for a beautiful country walk we get home without having noticed the smell of the clover, the swooping of the seagulls or the billowing white clouds dancing to their own rhythm.

> *We had a friend from California visit us in Devon. From the moment he arrived he started talking about the movie he had just produced. We took a boat trip and he talked about the movie. We walked through quiet country lanes and he talked about the movie. We went out to eat in the evening by the river and he talked about the movie! Each time we pointed this out to him he would pause, look up and acknowledge how beautiful were his surroundings, then a few minutes later he would come back to talking about the movie. When he left he expressed how much he had loved it, but we wondered if he had ever really experienced being here!*
>
> EDDIE

How often do we really listen or really see? Are we aware of the breath that enters and leaves our body? Life is precious, each breath, each moment. A healing into the moment. For we never know what is going to happen next. Just as we have got it

12

all planned and think we have it all worked out, it changes again! Yet we continue to cling to our plans and dreams. Are we able to come into the present moment and accept that what happens is a part of our learning process? Do we allow for a balance between our work and responsibilities and the ever-present beauty of life? If not, then what are we waiting for?

These questions point to basic attitudes that influence our whole way of life, thus affecting our healing. As we learn to celebrate each moment, we bring inspiration and warmth into our lives. What could be our purpose for being here if it is not to find joy and fulfilment as human beings, to learn to be at peace and see the preciousness of this human life? To discover the wonder and glory of being truly human. To reveal the beauty of our existence. Are we decorating and redecorating our home and yet not looking at our true home – this human body that is unconditional in its service to us? A heart that beats and sends nourishing blood throughout our being. The breath that oxygenates our cells. The organs that cleanse and maintain. The brain with its great intelligence. This wondrous home that allows us to explore endless depths within.

It is important, therefore, to ask what we want in life – deeply, not just superficially – and to discover our purpose. This may be as simple as deciding to work creatively with our hands, to serve food to the homeless, to go back to college and learn a new skill, or to be with those who are in need. What we do is an expression of our inner motivation. As we find our purpose we tap into an abundant source of creative energy, like a treasure hunt that goes ever deeper inward. We may have gone to discos and partied till the early hours, we may have travelled and seen the wonders of the world, but the greatest enjoyment is to be found in coming home to ourselves!

My real purpose is to forgive, not to dwell in the past or feel resentment towards others who have affected my life. And on awakening to think positively and even look forward to breakfast!

W.P.

13

TIME OUT: To Discover Purpose

Have some paper and a pen with you. Find a quiet space to be alone. Sit still and spend a few minutes relaxing, simply watching the flow of your breath as it enters and leaves your body (see p.42 for helpful advice on breathing). This helps you to become quiet. When you feel ready, ask yourself the following questions:

- When do I feel that my life is most meaningful?
- What do I enjoy doing most?
- What are my real priorities?
- What is the deepest purpose I would like to express in my life?

Let the questions sink deeper and deeper. There may also be other questions you want to ask yourself. Create the space to allow the answers to arise from an intuitive, feeling space. As words come, write them down. At first there may be a rush of words that are quick – mainly mental replies. Keep going, and let words come from a more free-flowing place inside you. It may not happen all at once, but whatever arises can be worked with. When you feel ready, ask yourself the following questions:

- What is it that is stopping me from bringing this purpose into actualization now?
- What needs to change in my life so I can express my purpose?
- How am I limiting the expression of my deeper feelings?

Again, allow plenty of time to let the answers arise from within. Write then down as they come. Finally, ask yourself:

- Is there at least one thing that I can commit myself to doing that will enable this purpose to begin to manifest in my life? What practical steps can I take, for instance, in the next two months towards fulfilling my purpose?

See if there are any other questions you want to ask yourself. Write your answers down and then make a commitment to putting them into action. This commitment is important; you will be able to draw new and added strength from it all the time. Let it grow like a seed freshly planted. In time it will flower.

IS WELLNESS OUR GOAL?

As we initiate this inner searching we may find ourselves confronting a related issue, that of whether we really want to be healed. This is not always a simple or obvious matter. Our difficulties and problems become a central part of our lives, giving us a reason for being, a cause for conversation and for attention. We begin to believe this is who we really are: through our difficulties we find an identity, even a sense of purpose. Holding on to them, we make them solid. Then our thoughts, actions and perceptions arise in relation to this central theme, limiting our ability to see beyond ourselves to a greater picture.

Margo told us everything was fine until her aged sister moved next door. Then her life became unbearable as this woman took over without any respect. But despite knowing, consciously, what she needed to do and say to remedy the situation, Margo did and said nothing, although she would readily complain to others. Her sister was, unconsciously, an important scapegoat for Margo's own problems. She would say that her life was fine if it were not for her sister. By blaming everything on someone else Margo did not have to see herself, nor did she have to deal with the realities of her own life; any problems were simply due to her sister's presence. This was not a conscious activity, but it was creating irritation for all the people involved.

15

The reasons for focusing on our difficulties are many, and invariably they are not conscious. It is vital that we do not blame ourselves. None of us consciously wants to beat ourselves up, to cause ourselves distress or to live in confusion, but unconsciously there may be hidden, obscure reasons for perpetuating such conditions. The practice at the end of this chapter is there to help you look more deeply at any hidden limitations you may have. If you look closely and honestly you will find them. For our stories are often remarkably similar – one person's pain or confusion is something we all may experience.

I am beginning to see how I fear losing loved ones, fear rejection, and that I don't trust happiness – as soon as I feel it I begin to doubt it and get scared I'll lose it again. I feel trapped in my fear and so I sabotage my own happiness. I never realised this before, how I cannot enjoy the moment for fear of the future. I want to change but I am scared to let go, feel too insecure, I fear an emptiness and loneliness.

PAUL DAVIS

I know I hold on to old patterns, ingrained physical and mental ways of being and old illnesses. I fear this although my greatest wish is to be free and healthy. This seems so illogical! I seem scared to move into new territory. And I hate it as it all seems so selfish and neurotic and pointless. I just want to let go but I don't know how.

JONATHAN GREEN

Just as with a child, when there is something wrong with us we are given extra love and attention, and perhaps now we are worried that becoming well means we will no longer receive that special love. Or perhaps our discomfort makes us feel like someone special, someone worthy of respect for all the pain and trauma we have endured. We want to make sure others know how much we have suffered!

There may also be a strange sense of dread at the idea of being without our difficulties, worries or concerns, for who would we be then? Have we forgotten what it is like to be any other way? Have we lost touch with who we are or could be without our pain? Would we remain lovable and desirable? Would there still be people admiring us, or offering us their friendship and help?

In confronting my healing I have the support of some very loving people who are always within reach to teach and encourage and support and love, but if I do get better and heal, would I still have as much support and attention? I have no grounds for knowing that I would have any less love and encouragement, but I fear rejection should I be free from the difficulties in my life.

ALICE BRYANT

Our difficulties may also be a way of getting back at someone for something that has been done to us, a way of making a lover or relation feel guilty. The relationship is maintained due to one partner being in need and the other partner feeling unable to leave.

Equally it can be a way of punishing ourselves for a past deed, a way of paying our dues: guilt pressing heavily upon our shoulders soon weighs us down. Or the thought of being healed can appear beyond our reach; it seems impossible that we could live with wholeness and peace, and therefore we stay in a state of agitation. When something good happens we don't trust it – we wonder how long it will last.

Have I the right to receive love from another human being? Can I allow someone to see me completely? What is stopping me from being whole is the in between bits – times when someone else sees all the garbage in me. I find this hard, I protect my garbage so no one can see it, but that means I don't have to deal with it either. So I end up living a lie, not being true to myself or to anyone else.

SHEILA JENKINS

Where physical problems are concerned, it has been shown in various research studies that, given the choice, many people prefer to have an operation than to change their behaviour, or want to be given medication rather than to confront their own anger or fear. In other words, when we disassociate the mind

17

and body we prefer to cure the body without healing our whole being.

This does not mean we should not have the operation or take the medication – such procedures are not separate to healing – simply that an illness gives us the opportunity to heal our lives on a larger scale. It is like an invitation to discover a deeper appreciation of life, a beauty in every moment, a richness in every smile.

As healing means to become whole, we therefore cannot heal just the physical without also involving the psychological and emotional. Each influences and reflects the others. Such healing means making changes, and change implies the unknown. Facing the unknown is a great challenge. Our upbringing, the problems we have had and mistakes we have made, all these and so much more may actually feel familiar and safe, despite the fact that they have caused us pain in the past. Old patterns die hard, we are reluctant to let go, for the past has led us to who we are now. Moving into new territory may feel scary in comparison as there are no well-trodden paths ahead, but it is deeply rewarding.

Is our desire to heal, to be fully alive, greater than any other desire? Do we have a choice? Do we have the courage to find that deeper level of healing and fulfilment that we so yearn for? We can go from one situation to another and see life as a burden, or we can choose to find our way to wholeness. Inner joy and peace are ours when we are willing to work with ourselves.

And this takes patience and honesty: it demands the faith that we can change, and the effort to see it through no matter what happens or how long it takes. The way becomes clearer when the things that used to be important lose their significance and a deeper understanding emerges. When the suffering and hopelessness of the human condition become too much to bear, then the longing for something more becomes too great to hold back.

As we turn to face ourselves, as we breathe and relax into ourselves, we discover that both love and compassion are there within us. While we are hiding from our reality, while we have our backs to ourselves, the heart is not seen and we cannot embrace ourselves with love. In resisting change we harden against the softness. If we surrender and let go of the resistance, then warmth can fill our being. Even when it appears that everything is falling apart – especially then – do we need the courage and faith to spread wide our arms and let the heart open. Faith can move mountains.

I was a swami in India, travelling with my guru, Swami Satyananda, on an All India Tour. It was a spring day in 1969 when an elderly man approached my guru to ask him to come to the man's home to see his ailing wife, to bring condolence, spiritual healing and any sense of hope he could instill. The man seemed convinced that, if a swami came, his wife would change for the better. This time my guru sent me in his place. I was in awe. Here I was, a young, shaven-headed swami, wearing simple orange robes and barefoot, going out for the first time on my own. I walked barefoot because, during the Tour, whenever I wore sandals and left them outside a home we were in, they would disappear. I had been living in seclusion from the world for the better part of a year, doing intensive meditation and observing silence. The little communication I had was with others who were also living in the ashram. Now I was to help heal someone?

We took a rickshaw, guided by a man holding the vehicle and running very fast. He took us into a village area and let us down in front of a mud hut. Upon entering I was greeted by a woman offering me bananas. A guest is considered to be sent by God and so is treated as such. With a visiting swami the custom is to offer fruit. As I took the bananas the woman cried as if she saw me as God. I walked towards the bed of the sick person and I could feel everyone was very relieved that I was there. No one could speak English and I couldn't speak Hindi, except for the odd word, but we communicated in gestures. The room was filled with a soft light, a peace and gentle silence. I found myself reciting the mantra OM NAMAH SIVAYA. At the time I didn't know what it meant. But everyone seemed satisfied and I left. They were all smiling as if I had performed a miracle. Their faith was overwhelming. Later I was told that OM NAMAH SIVAYA was a powerful healing mantra.

EDDIE

Creating a time for healing means making time to be tender-hearted with ourselves, to bring about a balance and enter into our purpose. It is about rejoicing in the moment and making all our moments worth living. It is about not being afraid to ask for help or for support. We can start by telling our loved ones that we love them, by being a friend to those who might need comfort, or by asking for a friend to be with us when we need comfort. We can move the furniture around in our home to create a new atmosphere, change our daily routine to include exercise and meditation, or perhaps add fresher and more wholesome foods to our diet, so that a healthier environment is created. By being flexible we let in a whole new way of being, creative ideas and images that encourage wholeness.

As we open to the healing, a peace permeates our being – a warmth and an ease. Through an acknowledgement of the pain come an acceptance and a growing relationship with ourselves. There will be times when everything feels OK, and other times when we might be wobbling! It is a gentle and tender process.

PRACTICE – Discovering Hidden Limitations

Take some time to find out where you are in yourself. This exercise helps you to see how you may be holding yourself back or limiting your self-awareness. Have some paper and a pen beside you. Sit comfortably and at ease, with your back straight and your eyes closed. You can lie down if it is easier.

Begin by focusing on the natural rhythm of your breath as it enters and leaves your body. Just watch the breath, breathing naturally, for a few minutes. As you do this the mind becomes quieter and more easeful. If your mind drifts, be aware of it drifting and bring it back to watching your breath.

Now acknowledge that you have a body: feet, ankles, knees, legs, fingers, hands, arms, back, front, neck, head. Feel your heart pumping blood throughout your system. Acknowledge this body that you spend your whole life in,

---

feel it as if it were a temple. Treasure this body. Treasure this breath that gives life. Know that to be alive is to have received an invitation to discover great riches. It is a wonderful gift.

Now focus on the part of your life you would like to heal, whether it be a physical problem, an emotional difficulty or a psychological issue – whatever it may be, bring this part of yourself into your mind. Just sit with an awareness of the issue, without judgement or fear. Just be with it, quietly, holding it in your mind. Breathe in and breathe out.

Then become aware of all the side-effects of this issue – all the ways it is affecting the rest of your life. Recognize the limitations and difficulties that you have to cope with because of this issue. Let the awareness of your breath keep you in touch with your body while you do this practice. Take as long as you need to explore the effect of this issue on your life.

When you feel you know it completely, begin to imagine you are free of the problem, completely free and healed. It is done with. For instance, if you are experiencing difficulties in your marriage, imagine you and your partner being loving and caring to one another. If you are hurting inside from past abuse, imagine yourself healed and able to forgive the person who abused you. If you were rejected as a child or as a lover, imagine yourself being welcomed, embraced and lovingly accepted by the one who rejected you. If you have a physical difficulty, imagine yourself without it, fit and well, being able to walk or run. Whatever the issue you are dealing with, imagine yourself free and healed. Imagine all the other aspects of your life that were previously influenced by this issue also being healed and released. If you feel blocked or tense when doing this, then remember to breathe in and out, gently. Breathe into the tension. Soften and relax your belly.

As you do this exercise, observe any feelings that arise in you. There may be feelings of resistance – that you cannot do this, that it is not possible for this healing to

21

happen, that there is too much pain. You may find it very hard to imagine. There may be feelings of anger and resentment, or of sadness and grief; feelings you do not want, or feelings you do not want to let go of. Remember to breathe in and out. You may alternatively feel light-hearted and happy, released and free. Whatever the feelings, acknowledge them fully.

Now begin to look at what might be stopping you from being in this healed state. Be as honest as you can. Above all, do not simply blame it on another person – that because of them you are unwell or unhappy and therefore cannot be healed. Make sure you are not being judgemental, getting caught up in who is wrong or right. In this experience you are only concerned with what is happening in you and what your own patterns of behaviour might be. Right now, no one else matters. Acknowledge and recognize and be gentle with yourself. You want to uncover those areas where you may be holding on to pain for obscure, unconscious motives, even though consciously you want to be healed. Try not to resist, deny or repress. Breathe in and breathe out, have a soft belly.

Look as closely as you can at those parts of you that say you cannot be well, cannot forgive, cannot be healed. Now write them down. Write down all the reasons that are resisting your healing, all the reasons that are holding you in pain. There may be many, or there may be only a few. Look as deeply as you can and be as honest as you can. Your healing depends on your honesty. Take as much time as you need.

When you have finished writing, take a deep breath. Hold yourself in a gentle embrace and know that you have started your healing. Honour this. Know that beneath the fears, anxieties, insecurities and confusion lies your healing; it is yours to embrace and rejoice. It *is* possible for you to heal and to be whole. This is who you really are; it is who we all really are.

2

OUR
GREATEST
OBSTACLE

*He that falls in love with himself
will have no rivals.*
BENJAMIN FRANKLIN

Invariably the first obstacle encountered as we begin the healing journey is ourselves. For although we want to be healed – want to have a healthy, loving and full life – the actual doing of it is another matter. It would be so much easier if we could just get from here to there without having to do the bit in between – the how-to stuff! Dr Bernie Siegel calls this our 'work', that which enables us to let go of here in order to get to there. And it *is* work: it does demand effort and time, there is no magic cure or way that it will happen without our conscious involvement. As the modern sage J. Krishnamurti said:

This is your life and nobody is going to teach you, no book, no guru. You have to learn from yourself. It is an endless thing, it is a fascinating thing, and when you learn about yourself from yourself, out of that learning wisdom comes. Then you can live a most extraordinary, happy, beautiful life.

So what is it that is stopping us? What is it that resists making changes, or releasing those things that aren't working and embracing those things that do work? If you did the practice at the end of Chapter 1, you may have uncovered some of the ways in which you are holding yourself back. You will have touched on some of the issues that are important and are affecting your life. Now you are confronted with what to do about them. Because they won't go away on their own, they need your help.

Making any sort of change can result in feeling vulnerable and insecure. When we make the big life changes such as getting married, moving house or starting a new job, then there is plenty of support and people sympathize and help. They have done it too – they know what it's like and how hard it can be.

Making the personal changes in life by working with our own issues is quite different. Family members and friends who have known us for a long time in a certain way can find it hard to accept that we are beginning to think differently, that we want to express our feelings more honestly or to confront hidden issues. This can upset the status quo, the way things have always been, even the social order itself. Others may not understand or will feel threatened by what the change means for them; some may even withdraw support or try to stop us. It is a new arena.

After years and years of fitting in and giving the right responses at the right times it seems dangerous to let them see me as I really am. If I become more who I really am, won't people say, 'Who does he think he is?'

SIMON GRAHAM

What is stopping me is not always being true to myself but rather conforming to other people's ideas of everyday living and what I should be like. If I am true to myself then I am challenging and threatening other people.

BARRY LITTLE

The changes we are talking about occur when we begin to clarify what we think and feel for ourselves and to define our own direction. This change is based on the irrational, the intuitive; it asks that we follow our heart, not our head, so explanations are not always easy. We may need to be tactful and gentle, not to make others agree with us, but rather to let them accept the changes in their own way. It is essential that we are true to ourselves, but also that we honour and respect the feelings of others.

The healing journey asks that we make a commitment, not to anyone or anything else, but to ourselves. To say *yes* to ourselves. As we proceed, all that is keeping us from being healed will arise – the fears, the uncertainty, the hurts and shame, the patterns of self-abuse or guilt, all the hidden agendas. It takes commitment, a real willingness, not to give in to these patterns but to keep working and growing, staying with the process and being a friend to ourselves. To allow the patterns to go without clinging to the past they represent.

In my late teens and early twenties I was deeply involved in Buddhist meditation and contemplation. In those years I experienced a profound awareness of my true self and love of silent solitude. I spent six weeks in solitary retreat, revelling in the absolute quiet. Then, at twenty-five, I found myself emerging into the world from both the order I had been involved in and from my first marriage. Inside I knew my spiritual self, but outside I was a lonely twenty-five-year-old looking for friendship. However, as I made friends I actually felt even more lonely; I had a yearning for a spiritual connection that was never quite fulfilled. No one knew what I had experienced and I knew no way of sharing this. I missed the discipline and commitment of the ordered spiritual life. I would compromise, taking long solitary walks or meditating in the early morning, then by night seeking out my friends. Eventually I began to feel like a traitor to my own cause. I was not expressing my spiritual heart in my life but allowing the pleasure/ pain syndrome to bury me. I was getting depressed. Eventually I hit crisis point. It caused me to stop, to turn myself inside out, to

25

reconnect with who I was. It was a healing of the chasm that was so desperately yawning. It was a coming home to myself.

DEBBIE

The strongest motivating force of life is to grow, as seen in a tiny acorn that can become a giant oak tree or a weed that comes up through the cracks along the roadside. This compelling drive to grow is within us too – it is our desire to become whole and it is reflected in our commitment to ourselves. Our body, mind, senses and feelings are the instruments that can be used to heal our wounds. Instead of being obstacles, our difficulties are the very opportunity we need to move ahead. But the motivation has to come from within us, from a place of honestly wanting to heal.

This much has to be our own responsibility. Certainly there will be others there to teach and guide us – fellow travellers offering support and laughter, those who share our ups and downs, teachers appearing in unexpected places – but the initial impetus has to come from within. When it does, the help we need will be there. As the poet and dramatist J. W. Goethe so eloquently said,

> Until one is committed there is hesitancy, the chance to draw back, always ineffectiveness. Concerning all acts of initiative (and creation) there is always one elemental truth, the ignorance of which kills countless ideas and splendid plans: that the moment one definitely commits oneself, then providence moves too. All sorts of things occur to help one that would never otherwise have occurred.

And this is where we so easily stumble! How hard it is to believe that it is possible, or that we are worthy, or that we deserve to be healed, that this is something viable and achievable. How much easier it is to put it off by saying, 'I could never really be at peace' or 'I've been this way far too long, it's too late to change now.' For every reason to move forward there is an excuse waiting around the corner ready to hold us back. It can seem like an endless uphill struggle. But if we believe in our heart that there is a possibility, just the slightest spark, a glimmer, of 'Well, maybe, perhaps I could try', then let us not hesitate. Nothing could be more rewarding.

TIME OUT: To Look at Your Commitment

Create some time to look within yourself, to see what you really need and what you may be ready to leave behind. Have a paper and pen to write down your feelings. Take a few minutes to sit quietly, watching your breath enter and leave your body. When you are ready, ask yourself the following questions:

- Am I really committed to being healed?
- Am I being honest with myself?
- Are the people closest to me being supportive?
- How important to me is their approval?
- Am I compromising myself in case I upset anyone?
- Is this OK?
- Do I feel unsupported by my loved ones?
- Have I really talked with them and asked them for support?
- Am I trying to make them change their life to be like me?
- Is it OK with me if they do not change?

There may be many occasions when compromise or the consideration of other people's feelings takes precedence over our own needs. This is fine. Giving and taking has a natural flow. But it is important to see the degree to which you may be using other people's feelings as the excuse for not making changes in your own life.

WHEN I HURT YOU, I HURT MYSELF

There are times when our own issues can be so demanding that we are unable to see how we affect others around us or even the world at large; the inter-connectedness and relationship between all beings, all life, does not penetrate. We get locked into our own space. Therefore I can insult you and walk away, so wrapped up in my own stuff that I am completely unaware of how wounded you may be. We hurt each other when we do not live with an awareness of our connectedness, when we are in separate, isolated worlds, where each is responsible only to themselves.

This separation creates the delusion that we can hurt someone else without being hurt ourselves, that our behaviour is of no relevance to anyone else, that we can even make other forms of life extinct without it affecting our own life. Suffering arises from this belief that we are all unrelated, that we need to fight and argue to prove we are right, that we need to be selfish, greedy or aggressive in order to survive. The lack of connectedness stops us from being receptive, loving and caring, even with those who are nearest to us.

My father always had a negative attitude towards me, never saying anything nice, always criticizing, never making any effort to be loving. We were rarely at ease with each other. In my late twenties I went to see him, wanting to explore and heal our relationship. He said, 'Why should I get to know you when there are thousands of other people I'm not bothering to get to know?' I replied, 'Perhaps because I'm your only daughter and you're my only father and we might find it interesting.' He said, 'How can I know there will be something in it for me? I answered, 'You can't. You can only try.' 'But why should I try when I'm not trying with all those other people out there?' And so it went on. I said how our relationship had influenced my relationships with other men, from early promiscuity to a failed marriage to a father figure. I was watching myself attracting pain in my relationships and desperately wanted to stop the pattern.

D.H.

28

Within each one of us there is a natural desire to be accepted and loved by others, to be affirmed and reassured. When this is denied or repelled it is equally natural to feel victimized, wounded or alienated and to try to win that love through acceptable behaviour. Children learn from an early age what will bring a reward and what will bring punishment; this attitude is then carried into our adulthood. A woman in one of our workshops told us how, by the time she was three years old, she knew how to use her body to get whatever she wanted. Others have expressed a similar awareness.

> *I suffered as a child! I was aware of shame, guilt, humiliation, fear and weakness. What I wasn't aware of was how much I tried to gain love and recognition by sublimated activities through achievement. I was angry and upset.*
>
> CHASKI

Rarely do we hurt or upset another on purpose, but the unconscious pain rises up and we react without real clarity or understanding. If our actions are hurtful, are they right? Are they skilful and meaningful? Do we need to reappraise and see our behaviour more clearly? Or do we feel out of control, a victim of circumstances, unable to do anything about the situation? Victimhood is intricately connected to feeling that we do not have any personal power. In *The Way Ahead*, Serge Beddington-Behrens explains:

> At its root, I see victim consciousness as a symptom of our feeling separate from life. . . We tend to give our power away, abnegating all responsibility for determining the course of our lives to forces outside of ourselves and, unconsciously or consciously, imbuing those forces with the power to hurt us in some way. In so doing the victim creates a space for the victimizer – those forces which would crush and suppress – to flourish.

> *I perceive my son as cold and withholding from me and I want him to be warm and open. What am I doing to stop him? Am I*

expecting him to be what he is not? And my daughter, who is so prickly and defensive and who I try to love but who irritates me so much! I am afraid of her, I think — I am afraid to confront her when she treats me unreasonably. I don't know how to cope with her nastiness. I want to point out how unnecessary it all is, but I feel powerless.

BILL PHILLIPS

What we are particularly concerned with here is how to heal this pain; how to find a place that does not react by causing more pain, but instead responds with understanding, patience and acceptance. Rather than feeling victimized or adding to the pain that is already there, we want to develop those qualities that embrace the human condition with compassion and tenderness.

For we are like drops of water in the ocean — individual drops, but simultaneously all part of the whole body of water. Nothing exists independently, separate from everything else. It is not possible. All things are irrevocably connected to each other. Thoughts, feelings, perceptions, desires — all are interdependent on and with all other things, interchanging and interconnecting in order to maintain, uphold and continue the life process. Our healing lies in truly understanding this. The Vietnamese monk Thich Naht Hanh states this beautifully:

> If you are a poet, you will see clearly that there is a cloud floating in this sheet of paper. Without a cloud, there will be no rain; without rain, the trees cannot grow; and without trees, we cannot make paper. If we look even more deeply, we can see the sunshine, the logger who cut the tree, the wheat that became his bread, and the logger's father and mother. Without all of these things, this sheet of paper cannot exist. In fact we cannot point to one thing that is not here — time, space, the earth, the rain, the minerals in the soil, the sunshine, the cloud, the river, the heat, the mind. Everything co-exists with this sheet of paper. So we cannot just be by ourselves alone; we have to inter-be with every other thing.

30

Knowing something intellectually is incomplete – it is only a part of the picture. The knowing must go deeper, beyond the intellect, into the heart and soul; it must come from our essence, the core of our being. Then the knowing is real and has relevance to our life. When we really know something then we are alive with it in every moment. Often when we say, 'But I know this!' it is the defence of the intellect, and we are not letting the knowledge enter into the depths of our being. The intellect works on a sense of rationality, yet life is irrational!

Essentially we are all simply human beings participating together in this planet. Different yet united: this is our shared humanity. The equality between us is the inter-relatedness. The content differs, not the essence. We can enjoy the differences and delight in the diversity, rather than letting this be a cause for conflict. If we make ourselves superior then we are making another inferior (and perhaps hiding our own deeper sense of inferiority), creating an artificial humility and insecurity. For in essence there is no superiority or inferiority. True equality is such a blessing, such a freedom from power plays and competition!

We had the joy of meeting with His Holiness the Dalai Lama in India. We were inside the palace, waiting on a balcony, beyond which rose the Himalayas, the morning sunshine catching the snow-capped peaks. As we went along the balcony we saw the Dalai Lama waiting for us by a further door. I immediately began to prostrate myself on the ground, this being the respected way of greeting a Buddhist teacher. But the Dalai Lama took my hand and made me stand, saying, 'No. We are all equal here.'

At first I thought, 'Oh, sure! You the great Dalai Lama, spiritual leader to millions, and me, an ordinary person. How can we possibly be equal?' But over the following months I took those words into the core of my being and experienced the true equality he was referring to. The equality of our shared humanness and simultaneously our shared divinity.

DEBBIE

31

THE REDUNDANT EGO

Realizing this essential oneness of all life confronts the ego – that which creates the idea of separation and cries out, 'What about me?', 'What about my feelings?', 'I don't care about anyone else, I just want to look after myself!' It is the ego that so longs to dismiss other people, that is not so concerned about their feelings but wants to find fulfilment and satisfaction for itself. Yet when we try to satisfy the ego we invariably end up feeling dissatisfied in a deeper place inside, for the ego can never be truly satiated. It is endless in its wants. Giving in to the ego and maintaining the separation and isolation that it demands rarely gives lasting joy.

However, it is not as if we have to get rid of the ego, or somehow kill it, but rather there is a softening, a releasing, an easing up on being so self-centred. To think we have to kill the ego is itself an egotistic act: *I* will kill *my* ego! Besides, it is not as if the ego is all bad or wrong. There is what we might call a negative or unhealthy side of the ego, but there is also a positive and healthy aspect of it.

The unhealthy ego is very demanding; like a child it needs constant attention. It is that which makes us think we are no good, that we could not possibly be healed – those self-effacing, self-centred, easily upset, destructive and despairing aspects of ourselves. We are not clever enough, pretty enough, attractive enough or nice enough to deserve a good life or to experience joy; since we are just a doormat, everyone might as well continue walking all over us. We lack confidence, self-esteem, and believe we are not worthy of anything meaningful. What difference does it make what we think or feel, for surely we are just a nobody and really not important?

The unhealthy ego believes we are worthless and blames the world and everything in it for creating its misery, but it has no interest in doing anything to promote well-being or healing, believing it is all far too hopeless. It will think of every excuse and way to corrupt progress and growth, highlighting what is wrong, never what is right.

This type of thinking is egotistic as it is so focused on self. The 'poor me' syndrome may be poor but is none the less very attached to me. Such a state is not to be confused with the genuine humility that arises as we see the interconnectedness between all life and how each is a part of a whole, unique but equal to all. And it is unhealthy because it holds us down and maintains a negative thinking frame. It is difficult to move out of such a mind-set – we all must know people who wallow in this mode for their whole lives. From such a place we cannot soar to great heights; we have to first find our way up and out before we can go further, to find ourselves and begin to feel good about what we find. To see what is right in ourselves and not what is wrong.

We establish a healthy ego by clarifying who we are and what our needs are, and when we gain more control over our life circumstances. There is a growing sense of belonging to the world, of having a role to play and a place to be. We stop thinking in terms of 'us and them', for we realize there is no enemy – we are not powerless. Confidence is building. Self-esteem is growing. We are redefining our identity, accepting ourselves more completely just as we are and discovering that it is not so bad to be 'me' after all. A healthy ego creates an environment conducive to growth and solid ground to walk on.

This is not the same as having an inflated ego where 'me' becomes greater and more important than anyone else – an inflated ego makes too big a deal about itself rather than recognizing a healthy relationship to the whole. Through activities such as becoming Mr Muscle Man, getting overly caught up in the drama and colour of past lives, or being a show off when performing amazing yoga asanas, the ego easily becomes puffed up and may lose touch with the real reason why we are doing such things in the first place!

There needs to be a balance. We are shifting from habitual conditioned behaviour, where we reacted without much thought or introspection, into a place of responsive self-awareness. The only drawback is in getting too self-involved. Unless we see the underlying humour in most situations, we can easily get bogged down by the clamouring of our egotistical self demanding attention! It does not like to be taken too lightly.

Charlie Chaplin said, 'Humour heightens our sense of survival and preserves our sanity.' We are all touched with a dusting of madness beneath the surface sensibility. The human condition is not always graceful and eloquent – it can easily be clumsy and garbled. If we take it too seriously, we lose perspective. Laughter releases the tension, allows a deeper level of relaxation, and, most importantly, means we recognize trivialities and do not get caught up in them.

> *I was sitting on the lawn talking to this wonderful unassuming Buddhist nun. She was from Yorkshire, very full of life and laughter. Jokingly, I said to her how soon we would all be in heaven and would get to see each other there. She agreed and said, 'Yes, and we'll look at each other and say, "What was all that about?"'*
>
> EDDIE

As the yearning for a deeper joy grows, and through developing awareness, compassion and service, slowly the ego becomes redundant. It happens naturally. In thinking of others, the ego dissolves into a loving and caring heart. The ego may even act as a stepping stone leading us to deeper truths and understandings, for a self-centred desire to improve and become a better person can actually lead us into healing unresolved issues. In India the ego is represented by a coconut, as it is the hardest nut to crack. It is offered to the guru as a sign of the student's willingness to surrender. When we let go of the ego we are letting go of our protective shell; then we can enjoy the sweet milk inside!

In the garden of gentle sanity
May you be bombarded
by coconuts of wakefulness
CHOGYUM TRUNGPA

34

I have always loved the image of a chick coming out of its shell. The shell must feel like cast iron as the chick tries to break it, pushing with its wings and beak. Our natural tendency is to help peel the shell away, but if we do that the chick will die. It needs the strength it gains from breaking its own shell. In the same way, sometimes the greatest gift we can give to others is to stand back and let them grow in their own way, to find their own freedom and not to try and do it for them. We can so easily see where someone else may need to grow, but each of us needs the space in which to grow by ourselves.

I was reminded of this one day in my early twenties. I was participating in an encounter group and we were doing some particularly intense communication exercises – sitting opposite someone and looking into our partner's eyes for long periods of time. It made me feel like my insides were turning to jelly, as if they were being totally exposed. There was nowhere to hide. Suddenly I felt cracks appearing all over me, like the cracks on an eggshell. I was breaking open, my protective covering was cracking wide and in that moment there was a glorious freedom!

DEBBIE

I LOVE MYSELF, I REALLY DO!

There is a fine distinction between being ego-centred and loving ourselves. While the egotist believes himself or herself to be the centre around which the world revolves, when we love ourselves we know we exist only in relation to all others; instead of being concerned only about our personal needs, there is an awareness that goes beyond our own presence.

Nor is loving ourselves necessarily about standing in front of a mirror and saying, 'I love you, I love you, I love you!' This does indeed help some people come to a deeper acceptance of themselves, but for others it can create even more tension, pain and resistance. Halfway through the last afternoon on one of our workshops, a woman suddenly burst out saying, 'I know I'm meant to love myself, but I just can't!' This is not what loving ourselves is about – it is not meant to create more pain.

35

Rather it's about making friends with who we are, feeling a connection deep inside to our inner being, the core of our humanness. It is about accepting ourselves just as we are and having an intimate relationship with each part, not just with the bits we like. Much of Western conventional upbringing has taught us that loving ourselves is immodest and wrong and too self-centred, when it is actually a necessary step along the way to healing. How can we be loved if we do not care about ourselves? How can we become whole if we are not embracing all of our being? How can we heal the wounds if we do not acknowledge they are there?

Loving ourselves is about breathing, feeling, accepting, allowing; about not holding on to the pain but believing, knowing that we can heal. It is about not having false images of who we are or putting ourselves in a box, but allowing the space to grow, move, to explore new directions. As the singer Tina Turner said, 'If you see yourself clearly, you can change anything.'

I was twenty-four years old and I had been involved with this woman for about three months when I decided to end the relationship. But she decided otherwise. For four long years she hounded me, waking me in the night by beeping her horn, endlessly harassing me on the phone, or driving me off the road. She would appear at parties and dump a bucket of ice over me or stub a cigarette out on my arm. There was no way I could stop her. Eventually I got ill with a thrombosis. As a result I realized I needed to change my life and start looking after myself. I got involved in meditation, improved my diet and began to heal. I discovered a friendship with myself, a deep acceptance of who I am. And suddenly the woman was gone. After years of fighting, she had stopped. I was no longer the person she had been relating to, the person she had been harassing. I had changed. The fight was over.

MALCOLM STERN

However, loving ourselves does not always come easily – it is not as simple as not being there one day and suddenly being there the next. It may take time and patience and the

36

willingness to fail. Years of pain or confusion are influencing us, pulling us back just as we want to go forward.

From an early age I was expected to serve and care for a mother who indulged in ill health. She liked me to dress as a nurse when I was ten years old. I may have been thanked at times but I never felt valued. This has stayed with me – the assumption, deep down, that I have no value and the basic attitude that I exist to be a servant of the needs of others. All this makes it very difficult to learn to love myself and to see my own value.

SARAH WILLIAMS

We can begin with a simple process of acknowledgement – taking time to experience our presence, our life form. To acknowledge it just as it is: this is who I am. Even this simple process of acknowledgement can open many doors if we have not connected so deeply before. It brings us into an awareness of our own being, of all that has gone into the making of ourselves. All the physical lumps and bumps, the psychological and emotional colours, textures, shapes, forms and patterns. The dark corners, the hidden recesses and the open spaces; the monsters and the angels.

Our responsibility is not to judge, not to discriminate or turn away from those pieces we do not like, but rather to see how each piece is a part of the whole and makes the picture complete, even if we do not especially like the finished product. Acknowledgement is not involved with right or wrong, with good or bad; it does not push away or deny, it does not judge but simply sees. Acknowledging ourselves is seeing who we are as we are. In *Chop Wood Carry Water* Rick Fields explains:

The necessary first step, then, is to acknowledge our present condition, even if it is (as it often is) one of confusion, hesitation and doubt. The acknowledgement is the essence of spirituality. It is a simple act, but only by this simple act – seeing where we are rather than imagining where we would like to be – can we begin the process of transforming all those things we usually consider stumbling blocks into the stepping stones they really are.

37

Once we acknowledge who we are, all that which makes us into an entirety, then we can begin the task of accepting. This again asks that we do not judge and discriminate, but simply hold in our hearts each different piece as it is and accept its role in the whole. If we push away or ignore any one piece, wholeness is not possible. The exercise at the end of this chapter will help you develop acknowledgement and self-acceptance.

To heal is to bring into conscious acceptance even those pieces that we are not particularly fond of, are maybe even ashamed of, that we want to deny or do not want to own up to. Acceptance is agreeing to be an adult, owning our own stuff and seeing the part it plays in creating the whole. Accepting ourselves means saying, 'OK, this is it, this is what is here.'

Do not push the pain away, it only makes it more painful. Do not push the anger away, it only makes more anger. Bring it into your heart. So you got angry, OK! Today you got angry for four hours – tomorrow do it only for three hours! Feeling guilty for getting angry is just adding more pain to an already hurting situation. Try not to make a big deal about it. Move on. Bring love to the pain, whether it is in the body, in the mind,or in the heart. Love will heal it much more quickly than will anger or guilt. As William Bloom says in *First Steps*:

> Nothing about ourselves should be unacceptable. Every dark, unpleasant, cunning, ugly and pathological aspect of ourselves is acceptable to us. If we cannot accept it, then we will never be able to transform it. If there are aspects of ourselves that we cannot accept and therefore cannot transform, then our whole process of spiritual exploration and transformation is flawed from the very beginning.

This implies taking each piece that we don't accept and holding it in our heart, embracing it into the whole. It means applying mercy and compassion to ourselves, as we have been and as we are now. Loving ourselves is not something that can be forced or pulled out of a hat, it comes through the effort we make in bringing each piece together. This involves our willingness, it brings us back to affirming our commitment to healing. We need to allow time just to sit down and explore our inner being, to enter into a relationship with ourselves. To find the places that are cold and isolated and ignored, and bring them into the warmth and light. To bring a tenderness and love to our fragility. This is best done in the peace and solitude of deep relaxation and meditation, as explained more thoroughly in Chapter 8.

When we take time for ourselves, whether for meditation, prayer or to be quiet, we experience a greater sense of objectivity and awareness. That is not possible while we are caught up in normal mental chatter – the criticizing, judging, insecurity, comparing, seeing things just from our own point of view chatter. In creating a quiet space we can observe what we are doing (see exercise on p. 44). To become whole we need to create this spaciousness in which we see ourselves more clearly.

If we do not take the time to work with ourselves, then those aspects which we are denying or repressing may eventually cause more suffering. We cannot resolve anything that we do not acknowledge or accept. If we sweep dust under the carpet, the dust is still there even if we do not see it. As we bring hidden issues into the conscious mind they can be released. They do not have to be analyzed – simply acknowledged and released.

There is an important difference between reacting and responding. Our normal action is a reaction: a habitual reply to a situation that comes from years of feeling the same thing in the same way. It is predictable, conditioned by those around us and how they too think and feel. A response is different. It comes from a creative and considerate place and is new in each situation. It is not dependent on others but arises from our own insight. To respond to a situation is to take responsibility – it is our ability to respond, to be sensitive, aware and caring.

THE SMARTIE TRICK

You might have heard about Party Tricks before, but this is the Smartie Trick, an essential ingredient for the journey!

If we buy a packet of Smarties (for anyone who doesn't know what Smarties are, we are talking about small, brightly coloured chocolate sweets) and we eat the whole packet at once, we may feel a little nauseous and perhaps also a little guilty for eating them all so quickly! About fifteen minutes later we may be wondering why we did it at all as the after-effects of the sugar rush kick in. Finally, we promise not to do it again, at least not for a long time!

However, if we put the packet in our pocket and we slowly eat just one Smartie at a time, we can pretty well guarantee that very soon the packet will be empty, but we will not be feeling nauseous or guilty. How could we, when we have only eaten one Smartie at a time?

The same approach can be used in working with ourselves and all the things we are trying to do – such as trying to love ourselves, overcome fear, meditate for an hour every day, forgive someone who wronged us, have an ideal relationship, and heal deep emotional or psychological wounds. If we try to do all of this at once it will soon become overwhelming; we will feel we can't do even one thing properly, that we are a failure, and so we might as well quit now and forget all about it!

For instance, John had been led to believe that all he had to do was love himself and everything would get better. So John tried to love himself. But no one had said anything about developing acknowledgement and acceptance first, so John started by saying, 'I love you' to himself, over and over again. And all his resistances arose, all the reasons why he couldn't and shouldn't love himself until, finally, he felt a complete and utter failure and simply gave up.

Going one step at a time, eating one Smartie at a time, means taking it step by step. It means being gentle with ourselves. Doing the Smartie Trick makes us Smart! We begin at the beginning and do not worry about the end. Perhaps we need to start with just fifteen minutes a day of meditation instead of a whole hour. Trying to do too much too soon may mean we end up doing nothing. It is like tending a garden, watering it, weeding it, caring for it, and seeing the flowers grow by themselves. We do not have to try to do everything at once. Know how much you can do and what feels right for you.

I used to care for the elderly. I had one client who did nothing but complain. Every time she opened her mouth it was to complain, whether about the food, the weather, her family – it didn't matter what the subject was, she would find something to complain about. I decided not to go along with this, so every time she complained I would say something nice.

'Terrible weather again.'
'Look at those delicate rain drops on the leaves.'
'Can't find anything to wear.'
'What a pretty dress you have on.'
'Food is rotten here.'
'Did you see that bird by the flowers?'

And so we went on. I never knew if I was having any effect until I went into her room one day while she was on the phone talking to her son. She was complaining as usual when she saw me sitting by the door. Immediately she said to her son, 'Whoops, Debbie is here, I have to say something nice now!' One step at a time!

DEBBIE

When we take things one step at a time then we cannot be a failure – there is no such thing – for everything that happens is a part of the journey, to be accepted and embraced. And many things will happen, resistances and fears will be encountered, doubts will be confronted, the wounds will make themselves known so they can be healed. By going one step at a time and taking it easy we can keep going, integrating the healing process into our daily life, dealing with each situation as it arises, one Smartie at a time.

Our greatest gift is not in never falling
But in rising every time we fall.

ANON

DON'T FORGET TO BREATHE!

We, the authors, have just three ground rules in our life. They have evolved over the years we have lived and worked together.

Ground rule No. 1: To be kind to ourselves, to be gentle. We are not here to create more pain. Rather than feeling guilty, shameful or bad, we chose to accept and be compassionate towards anything that might come up in our minds, at any time; we acknowledge and accept our basic humanity.

Ground Rule No. 2: No shoulds and should nots, oughts or ought nots! Rather than depending on being told how we should be thinking, how we ought to be behaving, what we should not be doing or ought not to be saying, we choose to ask ourselves deep inside what feels right for us. What feels appropriate, how can we best express our love, compassion and caring? This is not the same as 'anything goes', for it is based on a deep sense of natural morality and consideration for all beings as equal.

Ground Rule No. 3: Not to forget to breathe! Whenever anything is going on, tension is rising, distraction is beckoning, emotions are running high – breathe, with awareness. All times of the day, any time, we become aware and consciously breathe. The breath is the basis of our being, it gives us life and connects us to the life force of the universe.

The breath can be used in two main ways: by consciously remembering to breathe during difficult or emotional times, and thus to ease and relax the tension; and by focusing awareness on the natural flow of the breath, then witnessing anything that arises. Breathing is essential to the healing process. Obviously it is essential at all times, but here we mean conscious, aware breath, as opposed to our normal unconscious, automatic breath. We use this 'breath of awareness' as a way to maintain a harmonious relationship with ourselves.

Breathing with conscious awareness has an immediate and grounding effect, bringing us into the present moment. This is especially so during stressful times as the breath keeps us focused and relaxed. When we get tense or nervous, at times of trauma or fear, we usually take short, shallow breaths, high up in the chest. This creates more tension and keeps us at the edge. When we take a deep breath and breathe with awareness, in and out, then the tension eases. We let go of the resistance and sink deeper into our being. Then we are able to move more freely and consciously through the experience.

Just for a moment, stop and take a deep breath. Feel the breath all the way down into your belly. Let it out slowly through your mouth or your nose. Feel any tension going out of your body with the breath. Breathing in ease, breathing out tension.

Throughout the various practices suggested in this book you will see references such as 'remember to breathe', 'keep breathing' or 'become aware of your breath'. This is because conscious breathing will enable you to keep moving through the practice without closing up with resistance or fear. The same applies at all times of our lives, not just when we are doing a particular practice. Whenever we feel ourselves tense, pull back, react with fear or aversion, feel sad, overwhelmed, or choked with emotion, those are the very moments to remember to breathe deeply and consciously.

To work with the breath in this way encourages our healing into each situation. Breathing into the obstacles, the fear, the tenderness. We cannot heal if there is resistance or tension, for healing is a surrendering and softening into the feeling. Those emotions or blocks that are not constructive are limiting us from being alive in the moment. Breathing into these 'heavy' feelings relaxes and releases the tension that holds us in pain. Our friend Chaski says in a paper he wrote on pain:

I breathe into my vulnerability and commit myself to being in this place. Breathing is the mark of entry into this world for a baby and when it is cut off from the mother suddenly and is forced to depend on its own lungs, its own life support system, the baby will experience pain. Just imagine that – the first breaths of air searing into the lungs! This is what it can be like the first time we breathe into a vulnerable spot. So we need to commit ourselves to exploring that vulnerable spot without running and hiding, without denial.

A practice of simply watching the breath is the best-known and most traditional method of meditation. By sitting quietly and bringing our awareness to focusing on the natural flow of the breath, the rise and fall, the in and out, we deepen our understanding of ourselves. For in the process of doing this seemingly simple act, we have the opportunity to observe our minds going all over the place, like monkeys climbing trees, grasping at any distraction or creating internal dramas and dialogues. Then, as we become quieter, we find that beneath this mental chatter lie our wounds and defences which slowly come to light. In this way we get to see ourselves more clearly, observe or witness our issues, and can see what needs to be worked with. We use the breath to breathe into and through any tensions or resistances that may arise, thereby increasing our ability to soften into our healing.

PRACTICE – Loving Self

This practice is to help you become clearer about how you feel about yourself, how to accept those bits that you don't want to accept and how to develop a loving feeling for yourself. Have some paper and a pen nearby. This should be done sitting in a chair.

Begin by closing your eyes and watching your breath for a few minutes. Just watch it come in and then leave the body. Natural breath. Gently quietening the mind.

Now start to focus on yourself, and in particular the parts of you that you don't like or don't feel comfortable with, whether physical, emotional or mental. Dig deeply and honestly to find all those parts of you that you wish were not there or were different. As they become clear, write them down on the paper like a list. Take your time. Remember to breathe into any tension. When you have finished, take a deep breath and sit gently for a few minutes, letting your mind rest.

When you are ready, start to focus on those parts of you that you do like, that you do feel comfortable with. Begin a second list, opposite the first one. Don't be shy – nobody is going to see this! And don't be modest. Really acknowledge your good points and how you feel about them. This list is just as important. When you are done, take a deep breath. Sit gently and quietly for a few minutes.

Now start, one by one, to take each piece that you don't like or think you cannot accept and bring it into your heart. Simply hold that part of you in your heart and breathe into it. Does this part feel cold, lonely, neglected, unwanted, rejected? Can you bring it warmth? Can you see how this is a part of you, an integral part of your whole being, that it is not separate to you? That it needs and deserves to be loved as much as all the other parts. Allow an acceptance to grow. Hold it in your heart gently, lovingly, as you would hold a child.

Go through each item on your first list in this way. When you have finished this list, take another look. Has the first list become integrated into the second list yet? If not, then acknowledge that there are still bits to work on, still parts that need loving, need embracing. Know that you can come back to these another time, when you feel ready. Spend a few minutes remembering and rejoicing in your strengths. Take a deep breath and give yourself a big hug!

3

EMBRACING
FEAR WITH
FEARLESSNESS

It's about walking through that world of fear
so that you can live in a world of love.
BRUCE SPRINGSTEEN

My mother died five days after I was born. In the last few months of her pregnancy there was only a 50/50 chance she would live. She had a goitre and in those days they did not know about iodine or other cures that are used now. So I was born through a woman who knew she was dying. Nine months after her death my father married my mother's single sister as a way of keeping the family together. Then, when I was fifteen years old, my stepmother-aunt died. We had an argument the night before. She kept us up all night screaming, gasping for air, and was then rushed to hospital.

After a few hours the telephone rang, a stranger's voice telling us that she had died. I went running into the kitchen and in the horror I remember picking up a sharp knife and putting it to my stomach to stab myself. I couldn't do it but I wanted to. It was so painful, I was so afraid, I felt so alone. If only I could say, 'I love you' just once more!

Often in my life since then I have felt a deep fear which at times would engulf me – a fear of being alone, abandoned, left, that there was no solid ground beneath my feet, nothing that I could depend on. I have felt insecure, needing other people to give me assurance and affirmation. Life has had an emptiness, as if there was something missing that I could never quite define, and I have constantly searched for this. The fear held me back from making any emotional commitments, for there was the fear of being left alone.

EDDIE

Bringing confusion and anguish in its wake, fear comes in all shapes and sizes, each with the power and ability to hold us in an uncomfortable, awkward and confrontational state. Yet it is also a constant source of entertainment. We revel in horror films or paperback thrillers, watch news of wars and famine, and flirt around the edge of dread and terror. On the one hand fear is something we want to avoid, and yet it also fascinates us; we invite it in, then wish it wasn't there.

Fear can rule and destroy lives, families and countries. It is constricting, limiting, creating denial and repression. There are so many kinds of fear: the child fear, the teenage fear, the I-lost-my-job fear, the rape fear, abuse, birth, sickness, old age, loss of a friend or a loved one. The endless fear, the madness fear. The why-don't-you-love-me fear, the worthless and I'm-not-good-enough fear. The ugly and the meaningless fear. The I-can't-go-on-any-more and the why-not-die fear.

I fear giving up being special; fear giving out so much that I will have nothing left; fear being a victim to other people's needs and demands; fear relationships, commitment to others; fear emptiness. I feel engulfed by fear.

P.W.

Fear is a deeply primal energy that arises in relationship to survival, when what we believe is threatened and the ground we are walking on becomes shaky. When we feel there is nothing we can hold on to with any sense of security. There is

47

the immediate fear that arises when our lives are being threatened, and the imaginary fear that arises when we believe or think something fearful will happen some time in the future. The fear of the dark, of the enemy, of being out of control, of poverty, of being rejected, of being alone and of death. These fears appear real even though they may have no substance. We guard our world against the unknown, seeking out those who act and think as we do, rejecting those who differ from us. Fear controls the mind, pushing us into isolation, destruction and turmoil. The peace activist, Satish Kumar, says in his autobiography *No Destination:*

> For me there is no such thing as evil. There is only fear and ignorance. Wars and weapons are born from fear and ignorance. I found fear in Moscow and fear in Washington, fear in Paris and fear in London. The enemy is neither Russia nor America. It is fear which is the enemy.

Attending one of our workshops was a pregnant woman. Jilly was immersed in a great fear of death. She had some cause for concern as an emergency caesarean had had to be performed during the birth of her previous child. Jilly was terrified it would happen again. She also remembered her mother dying and not being able to say she loved her before she died. She wanted to see her mother now and tell her that things weren't all right, and how she felt so full of fear. Jilly had come up against an invisible wall of fear that she felt unable to penetrate. A tight energy that made her feel locked in pain. Her breath was short and shallow, creating further tension and stress.

When our energy is consumed by fear in this way we cannot move, our defences come down and we are rendered powerless. Fear is numbing. Our hearts close, not letting anything or anyone in and not letting our feelings out. We don't know in which direction to turn. Everything seems to be telling us that ahead lies unsafe territory, unexplored, new ground – do not enter. The fear becomes solid and locks into our bodies, like prison bars around us beyond which we cannot move.

As a child of four I sat, night after night, in terror watching
searchlights combing the skies and planes bombing Coventry, just
across the fields. This did not give me much confidence in a world I
could trust.

MUZ MURRAY

Fear is the ego's instinctive response to any form of threat to itself. If we cannot cope with fear it becomes overwhelming: then we are a slave to it, a victim of fear itself. We hear people say, 'I want to change but I'm frightened', not realizing that change is the very nature of existence and that when we fear change then we limit our healing. However, perhaps it is not so much fear that causes the problems, as how we deal with it. For fear has to be addressed in every moment and at every step along the way. Resistance is like a detour to a dead end: it makes movement forward into new places impossible. Fear can be totally debilitating, holding us in complete limbo and leaving us unable to move; or it can be a stimulus for us to push forward into new territory, a motivation to discover who we really are.

The biggest fear for me was when my husband left me for another
woman. Becoming a wife, mother and grandmother and being a
daughter and sister were all parts of life I had experienced.
However, becoming a divorcee, a single person after twenty-two
years of marriage, was a very scary experience. I was overwhelmed
by feelings of anger, hurt, bitterness, loneliness and fear. But I
used these feelings to help me through the transition. Such pain
and vulnerability gave me a certain kind of strength. Surviving
and getting through each day was tremendous.

PAT ASMAN

Take a moment to trace your life back: look at the innumerable times fear presented itself and how you met it and then moved on. Fear has always been there, we have always been confronted with it, faced it. The first time your mother left you alone, your first day at school, your first big exam, your first date, moving away from home, your first job. The list is endless. The fear arises, we meet it and later realize we have

49

moved beyond it. For fear is the entrance to a new experience, a new arena, the signal that change is underfoot. Eleanor Roosevelt, wife of former US President F.D. Roosevelt, said, 'You gain strength, courage and confidence by every experience in which you really stop to look fear in the face. You are able to say to yourself, "I lived through this horror. I can take the next thing that comes along." You must do the thing you think you cannot do.'

One day in the late 1960s, while serving in the RAF, I was called upon to carry out some work in the bomb bay of an aircraft of the V-bomber force which was on Quick Reaction Alert, armed with a nuclear weapon. This meant crawling a little way into the bomb bay itself and lying on my side alongside the bomb. Being near it made my scalp tingle. I was filled with trepidation at what I had to do. As I turned over to work on my other side, I kicked one of the side panels of the bomb with my foot. I was terrified! But it just made a metal sound as if I had kicked my car, and I suddenly realized that it was completely inert. It gave me a chance to see how fear can be so insubstantial. It helped me see my fear for what it was.

BILL FEENEY

TIME OUT: To Look at Fear

Have a paper and pen with you. Take a few minutes to become quiet. Focus on your breathing. Take your time. When you are ready, ask yourself the following questions. It does not matter if you cannot answer them all: just let the answers arise naturally.

- Are my fears based on reality or on what might happen?
- Have I been carrying them a long time, perhaps since childhood?
- Where did they originate from?

50

- Did I create them?
- Do they feel heavy?
- Is a particular part of my body affected by this?
- What would I like to do about them?
- How would it feel to let them go?
- Do I want to look closer and see if they are ready to leave?

Write down your answers. Ask yourself any other questions that come to you. Do this regularly, perhaps once a day or once a week, and see if your answers begin to change. Fears easily become repetitious – they grow into habits. We get used to feeling this way; then we don't know how to release the fear because we actually feel safer with it than without. But as we shine a light on fear, begin to name it, observe it and sit with it, then we see fear for what it is and can move through it more easily.

FACING THE MONSTERS!

When I was a child I had monsters under my bed. They were nasty monsters with big teeth and there was simply no way that I could get out of bed while they were there. If I did, then I knew they would grab my ankles. The only way I could get out of bed was to call my mother in and have her turn on the light. Then the monsters would recede into the distant netherlands and I could get up. Of course, if I then looked under the bed all I would see was a pair of shoes or perhaps an old teddy bear, but in the dark those monsters were real.

DEBBIE

Monsters – those parts of our being that we cannot reconcile and we wish would just go away. They get pushed into the underworld of our mind. Fears turn into monsters. Guilt turns into a monster, as do anger and shame. John Bradshaw explains how shame says, 'What I did was wrong', while toxic

51

shame says, 'I am wrong.' That's a big monster. Such monsters limit our actions and we are unable to move freely. They drain our emotions, our energy. We cannot love freely for fear of being rejected or hurt; we cannot give for we have not yet forgiven and the pain is still locked inside. We fear being taken advantage of, we cannot let go and trust, for our insecurity dominates with doubt. The monsters inside hold us back; we are bound by them.

> *In many fairy tales there are stories about the existence of a wonderful Treasure which the hero or heroine is trying to find. This symbolises our true self. However, discovery of it is never that straightforward as this Treasure is guarded by a great monster, a fierce dragon. But the dragon is also us! The only way to claim the Treasure or really find ourselves is to be brave and big-hearted and skilful and loving and humble enough to defeat the dragon. And this takes time and a lot of training and emptying, as dragons are pretty cunning and thick-skinned creatures!*
>
> SERGE BEDDINGTON-BEHRENS

When we begin to look into ourselves it can appear as murky and fearful territory. There are unconscious or unresolved issues here, things that are repressed, hidden and denied. It is never easy to face the demons. They look so big, so oversized, that they seem impossible to deal with. Even when we try, it feels as if we are getting nowhere fast.

Debbie recalls participating in a therapy group in her early twenties and really feeling as if the issue she was confronting and wanting to heal was being solved, only to find it erupting into her life again some years later. It is not as if we are getting nowhere – each step *is* a step towards healing – but there are many layers that go deep within and it takes time to uncover them all, one by one. If we don't put an evaluation sticker on how well things are going, but just go one step at a time, then breakthroughs do happen: the light does appear at the end of the tunnel.

> *In my self-exploration, I realised I had to learn to see my fears and hostilities and anti-life emotions for what they were; I needed to*

confront all those parts of me which I had spent so much of my life denying and projecting on to others. And underneath all this, I began discovering little nuggets of love which then gave me the inspiration to delve a bit deeper. Shadow work, then, became inseparable from Heart work.

SERGE BEDDINGTON-BEHRENS

Repressed and ignored feelings stockpile in the recesses of the mind from where they wield great influence over our emotional freedom. Locked in the darkness, they become shadowy monsters that emerge when we begin on the journey and are wanting to heal. As love and fear are so intimately connected, the shadow often finds expression by creating a fear of love and of sharing loving feelings. Expressing love is an act of fearlessness, of open-heartedness, but revealing the fullness of the heart can leave us feeling vulnerable and exposed. So by treating love as a wishy-washy emotion we are saved from having to face our vulnerability. For instance, conventional male conditioning says if you are seen to be affectionate or over-emotional then you are not being 'man' enough. The body language of such an attitude expresses a fear of touching, of being close, of showing tenderness. There is a wall of defence that cannot be penetrated.

William told us how he had never shed a tear. He was in his late forties and had never done so even though he ached to cry and let his heart pour open. During a healing visualization (as on p. 98) he discovered the area around his heart to be like a black wall. Penetrating that wall William found a memory of a particularly scary moment at school when he was a young boy. His mother's words were ringing in his ears: 'Brave boys don't cry!' And so William didn't cry; instead he blocked out the fear and made a wall around his heart so he couldn't feel what was there.

Michael, a product of the public school system, told us how he had been taught to hide his emotions by showing the opposite of what he was actually feeling. If feeling happy, he was told to pretend to be indifferent, uncaring; if feeling sad, then he should pretend to be cheerful and happy. On no account should he show his true feelings. It was wonderful to watch both these men expressing their feelings to the group at a workshop.

> *Sometimes facing our monsters can raise a few eyebrows. We had given a talk in a Unity church in Colorado about facing our monsters and having the courage to confront that which is difficult or painful. Afterwards quite a few people came up to ask questions or speak with us. In the midst of this I found myself shaking hands with a gentle, quiet man – he looked as if he might work in a bank or as a NASA scientist – but whose name tag said 'Linda'. I commented on this being an unusual name for a man, and he replied, 'Well, I'm beginning to face my monsters!' I looked more closely and saw that he had on some pale blue eye shadow and that, beneath the very ordinary grey shirt and plain beige slacks, he was wearing a pair of low-heeled woman's black patent shoes!*
>
> DEBBIE

JUMPING IN, FEET FIRST

It is the willingness to embrace our fear, in spite of resistance and denial, that stimulates our healing. The willingness to let go of the old, of the habits that bind, of the conditioning that tells us, 'No, don't, I am too afraid.' The head and the heart battle it out: the head saying, 'No, I am too fearful', the heart saying, 'Yes, I can do it', encouraging us to jump in.

> *The principal of the art college simply said, 'Sorry, we have no places left. You'll have to come back next year.' Inside I panic, I have to do this. I reply, 'Well, I'm sorry too, but I won't be leaving the building until you've given me a place on one of your courses.' He looks surprised. I look calm, intent. I feel afraid. I wait for seven hours. He pops out periodically to check whether I'm still there. Every hour I get stronger. My fear recedes. Finally he tells me, 'Someone has just cancelled on a two-year photography course. Do you want the place?' I smile and say thank you. I am elated. My heart is beating a little louder than usual. I'm glad I can hear it.*
>
> YA'ACOV DARLING KHAN

We become fearless when we take the first step of looking at our fears with a loving heart, simply examining the options and checking them out, without judgement, just seeing and acknowledging what is there. Seeing the fears that cause obstacles to healing, that keep us locked in pain and suffering. Deeply acknowledging them and being honest. Remembering always to breathe! Take a moment to ask yourself:

What is it in myself that is resisting being free?

Am I fearful of letting go?

Can I trust myself?

Do I fear what it would be like to be without fear?

Breathe into these questions. You may not be able to answer them immediately. Let them act as a stimulus to look deeper within yourself.

It was a dark, drizzling evening when I first went up the path to the ashram. I knew I would be confronting myself. It was the very first time I had been to a meditation centre. I felt sick in my stomach. I just wanted to run away. I found myself in a room full of people sitting on the floor and I couldn't breathe. I had a meal given to me but I couldn't swallow because of the lump in my throat. The people there were obviously well aware of me and were very loving. After dinner, there was a meditation that focused on the heart. I had to keep sighing to stop myself from crying.

We had silence from then until after breakfast the next day. I did not want to be there, I thought I already knew everything I needed to know about myself and all I wanted was for it to be morning. When it's light your mind can be distracted from itself, but when it's dark you are on your own. I felt lost, lonely, sick and frightened and wished I had never come anywhere near the place! In retrospect I was like a baby curled up in bed having helpless baby thoughts.

I obviously had to experience this as I actually got from the weekend exactly what I needed. Slowly the next day unfolded and I found myself relaxing, letting go. I found I wasn't alone. I learnt that it was OK to cry. What a relief! It was a very important step of my journey.

PAT ASMAN

For our healing to deepen there has to be a shifting from those patterns of behaviour that are maintaining pain to those that support and stimulate wholeness. Change is the very essence of life; when we move with it then we flow with life's energy. It is when we hold back the fears that limitations appear.

We do not know how we will be when we change – what will happen, how we will feel, what we will want to do. Looking at the future from where we are now cannot give us a clear idea, for when we change we will no longer be the same person. We will be different and our view will be different. Each moment is different. But deep within there is a knowing that it is right. Change is needed, just as winter leads to spring and to summer. As we go through the changes there grows a feeling that we are getting closer to who we really are. It is an adventure, a mystery that unfolds. What is necessary is not to resist, but to be open enough to welcome change and see what it has in store – the beauty and marvel of it all.

A rabbi asked recently, 'What is change? What really makes personal change?' My sense is that surrendering to the way our life wants to flow, allowing the fierceness of our desire to live our lives fully, to be who we really want to be, to outweigh the horror of the unknown, the fear of the emptiness of the space that must be there for a moment before a new pattern forms, to trust. These moments, these I do's, are the quantum jumps, the more visible signs of our change, and they are built on the slow tide of awareness that leaps up to them and follows them.

SUSANNAH DARLING KHAN

When we bring the monsters out of the dark and into the light, we see them for who and what they are. To do this we may need someone to help us: a mother, friend, counsellor or teacher. Monsters only appear as monsters when we give them our power, when we put time and energy into thinking about them. Facing our monsters by bringing light to them, we find they are actually not so ferocious after all, we are even able to make friends with them. They are only monsters when hidden in the dark. In the light they are not so bad – just a pair of old shoes or perhaps a lost teddy bear! Manageable, acceptable, not nearly so difficult. The nature of fear is to hold us back, to stop us from moving forward, but this can be transformed if we have the courage to turn around and face it. As a wise old Tibetan sage advised, we can invite our fears in to share a cup of tea!

There is a wonderful story of a man who falls off a cliff. As he falls he grabs hold of a branch, which then begins to break. Hanging there, clinging to the breaking branch, the ground hundreds of feet below him, the man starts to call out: 'God, help me, please! Help me, God! Please help me!' Over and over he calls for God to help him. Finally he hears a great voice booming, 'This is God. Trust me and let go of the branch.' The man pauses in thought. Then he calls back up the cliff, 'Is there anyone else there?'

SURRENDERING OUR HOLD

Being able to do what is asked of us involves our ability to surrender. We are being asked to surrender our defences, resistances, fixed ways of doing things, fears, old patterns, habitual behaviour – all this and so much more seems like it has to go. Everything except our common sense! And at first it may feel a bit overwhelming and all too much and would everyone please leave me alone for a while?

However, surrender is not about losing control, being overcome, giving power away or letting others take over, or about becoming a doormat for all and sundry to walk on. Surrender is about letting go of that which is holding us back from healing and releasing those parts of ourselves that are limiting our relationship with wholeness. Surrender is allowing the natural flow of events to unfold without resistance, without holding on to preconceived ideas on how life is or should be.

One evening, in a group therapy session, I connected with my ability to survive. I was only about twenty years old at the time but I already knew I could survive, no matter what happened. It was no problem for me. I felt very secure in my ability to survive, very confident, it was a way of being that I was used to. I had no doubts that I would be OK. But then I was asked what was the opposite of survival. And I hit this big hole. For me the opposite was surrender, was being vulnerable, and I had no idea how to do that. It felt alien, frightening, the ground was gone from under me and there was just this big hole that I knew one day I would have to jump into.

It took a few years to make that leap. To have the courage to start exploring my vulnerability, not to cling to my survival tactics but to let trust and surrender come in. I would test the trust to see if it worked, that if I let go of control things would still happen, and it was OK. But it was scary. Being vulnerable, to me, was all tied up with being weak and unable to cope. How would I survive? But most importantly it was connected to letting others in emotionally, allowing intimacy, and my wall of protection took a long time to come down. The beauty was that as I breathed into it and allowed myself to let go, to surrender, I found I was actually happier, it became easier and more enjoyable than trying to stay in control.

DEBBIE

Through surrendering our resistances we turn destructive patterns into constructive ones. Surrender teaches us how to let go of attachments so that the old is free to drop away. By becoming aware of our habitual reactions – rather than giving in to old patterns of behaviour – we see what new responses there may be, arising from a more aware and creative place within us.

Practising surrender means being able to release the fear or need to control if a situation is not going as we would like it. Remembering to take a deep breath, we can quietly wait to see what happens rather than blindly jumping in. Surrender is about not always having to be right, but seeing that there may be other ways of being and doing that are equally valid to our own. It is paying attention and being sensitive, allowing things to happen without our need for manipulation. It is a softening and releasing, a letting go of one moment as we enter into the next.

In surrender we discover our vulnerability, our tender heart, the beauty that we mistake for hopelessness or weakness. Vulnerability is the raw beingness beneath the superficiality, beneath the mask behind which we hide, fearful that anyone will see us or know us for who we really are. How many people wear their fear openly, are able to admit that they are fearful? Yet who isn't, at some time or another? Being vulnerable does not leave us brittle and easily broken, but soft and gently open, flexible, more alive.

> *Some years after first connecting with my fear of vulnerability I was participating in a bioenergetics group where we were exploring the bodymind relationship. One by one we each had to stand naked in front of the group. The group would then 'read' our body, seeing where we were holding areas of pain and trauma, like a woodman 'reading' the life of a tree. This was videotaped so we could later watch ourselves at the same time as hearing the analysis. As I stood there, totally exposed and feeling horrendously vulnerable, I also sensed the love and support from the rest of the people. I was in a safe place. I took a deep breath and let go into the vulnerability. And it was OK. Later, watching the video of myself, I saw this strong, capable body. And I saw inside it this swirling pattern of softness and tenderness and gentleness.*
>
> DEBBIE

If we can watch our fears, then they will show us the areas where we need to work: we will be given a clear picture of our weaknesses. Through surrendering those fears, one step at a time, we connect with who we really are, with the deepest levels of strength and knowingness within that support us on the healing journey. It is this relationship that gives purpose and direction: a trusting relationship with ourselves, a working relationship, a fearless relationship. Releasing that which is holding us back from such a relationship is essential.

EMBRACING FEARLESSNESS

By recognizing fear when it arises, but none the less continuing to go forward, we reduce the power of fear and enter into fearlessness. When we fear something and allow that fear to hold us back, then we are giving it power. In the process we become powerless. It stills our energy. Trying to deal with fear head-on may simply create more tension and barriers and not necessarily eliminate the cause of the fear. However, we can deal with it by coming into the heart. This is where we find fearlessness. By focusing in the heart, we can embrace our fear. The practice at the end of the chapter will help you with this.

Debbie likes to compare fear to the large and somewhat wild black bull that charged at her and a friend one day while they were out walking in the Welsh hills. There was nowhere to hide or run to, not even a blade of grass big enough! Debbie found somewhere by hiding behind her friend. He breathed deeply and opened his arms by his side, palms upward and gazed at the oncoming bull. It was this ability to enter into his fearlessness that finally turned the bull away.

Bulls come in many shapes and many colours: sometimes they charge from the front, but more often they sneak up from behind! They are the moments when something confronts us and we realize that we have nowhere to go, that running and hiding will make no appreciable difference. In that moment we are given a choice. We can either hide and pretend everything is OK, knowing full well that we are simply delaying the inevitable confrontation to a later date; or we can breathe very deeply and, despite the trembling, fearlessly enter into the fear, courageously step into the arena, and sink into our tender-heartedness and vulnerability.

I had a powerful phobia about hospitals and blood. It was a phobia that I had had for years and it always rendered me helpless. My therapist suggested I do hospital voluntary work. At first I froze when I thought of it, but the seed was planted and it grew. No easy way out of facing fear – I became a very frightened hospital volunteer for about six months. Then slowly I began to realize that I was actually enjoying my visits, that I was even helping patients to talk about their fears! That was two years ago, and visiting the hospital is now a regular high point of my week. From being a helpless divorcee with grown up children, to having Chronic Fatigue Syndrome, I now garden, swim, visit hospitals, do watercolour painting, go to healing and meditation groups, and I have even learnt how to speak in public, which meant facing yet more fear. I am beginning to understand the meaning of fearlessness!

PAT ASMAN

Fear is a contractive state, one that excludes and pushes away. It dominates the mind, leaving us frightened and powerless. Fearlessness is the opposite – it is an all-embracing state that includes all other conditions, accepting them, holding them, giving them courage and strength. Fearlessness is an expression of the heart. By breathing into the loving heart we draw fearlessness up and into action. This takes the steam out of fear: by embracing it we are disempowering it.

Love is letting go of fear. Where fear contracts, love embraces. Fear is all-consuming, it obliterates all other experiences. Love embraces fear, can hold it as the sky holds the rain. Love and fear go beside each other, like the sickness and the remedy. In *Grace and Grit* by Ken Wilber, his wife Treya says:

> I will bring the fear into my heart. To meet the pain and the fear with openness, to embrace it, to not be afraid of it, to allow it – this is what is, this is what is happening. This is the suffering we know all the time, constantly changing, changing. . . I'm not trying to 'beat' my sickness; I'm allowing myself into it, forgiving it.

In the heart we find the faith, trust and confidence needed to release the hold that fear has on us and to embrace it with compassion. For love embraces our human weaknesses, and in the embracing these weaknesses can develop into strengths. Love allows the fear to arise and holds it gently. Therefore, through fear, we enter into our wholeness and a deeper awareness of love.

I was doing a lot of meditation and introspection while living in a spiritual community in New York City. I needed a break from the city and wanted some open space, so I decided to take a ferry boat ride. While I was on the boat, on my way to the Statue of Liberty, it

61

happened in a flash, out of nowhere. I was suddenly experiencing universal love, a love that exists on its own, without reference points. It was a powerful realization. Everything dropped away and I could feel this all-embracing love. I saw love as the source of all things. A new way of being that stayed. It allowed me to confront fear — all the many different fears that would arise, unexpectedly, as fear seems to do — with an inner love, so that I knew I could bear it and could go through anything.

EDDIE

The physical posture of fearlessness is one of standing with our arms open, ready to embrace, hands by our sides with the palms facing forward. It may look weak and defenceless because all our most vulnerable organs lie unprotected, but the strength is in the openness. The posture of fear is one of cowering, with our fists clenched and our arms closed or wrapped around ourselves. It may protect our organs but it leaves us psychologically weak and defenceless – it exposes our fear in the need to be protected.

To be fearless is to have the willingness to explore ourselves, to acknowledge when we may be wrong and to express love tenderly. This is being a warrior of the heart – one who fearlessly travels uncharted waters through the ocean of consciousness. The tools of such a warrior are those of courage, acceptance, love, compassion and gentleness. These are used to break through the barriers of delusion, greed and hatred, to traverse our inner world and heal the wounds.

To be a fearless warrior requires perseverance and fortitude. The ability to be brave in the midst of fear. Instead of giving into fearfulness we breathe into fearlessness and keep going. Just as a mother holds her child in comforting, loving arms, we can hold our own fear as if it were a child, with love and trust. The singer Bruce Springsteen experienced this the night his son was born:

There's a world of love and there's a world of fear and it's standing right in front of you and very often that fear feels a lot realer and certainly more urgent than the feeling of love. The night my son was born I got close to a feeling of

62

real, pure, unconditional love with all the walls down. All of a sudden, what was happening was so immense that it just stomped all the fear away for a little while and I remember feeling overwhelmed. But I also understood why you are so frightened. When that world of love comes rushing in, a world of fear comes in with it. To open yourself up to one thing, you've got to embrace the other thing as well.

Being fearless means going beyond the illusion that things are solid and permanent and lasting. We are not solid, we are not permanent. Our thoughts are not solid. Fear is not permanent. Even Jesus said, 'And this too shall pass.' To be fearless is to go deeper, to see beyond the limitations. To realize that all things go through a process of creation, preservation and destruction. Even in this moment, this particular thought has arisen, is there for a moment and dissolves. Our breath arises, stays, then dissolves. Everything is in a process of being born, living and dying: our thoughts, our problems, our feelings, our fears. If we just stop and look, carefully, we will see how everything is in constant change. Nothing remains the same.

As we see this we awaken to an acceptance of the way things are. This is the healing that is our birthright. It is the discovery of our essential oneness, the purpose for our life. As the philosopher Plato said, 'We can easily forgive a child who is afraid of the dark; the real tragedy of life is when we are afraid of the light.'

PRACTICE – Embracing Fear

This practice can be done by either watching your thoughts and behaviour in everyday life and then reflecting back and seeing how fear arises (writing your observations in a journal is very helpful); or it can be done in a meditative state, where you are watching, witnessing and releasing your thoughts as they arise. Both procedures are offered here.

63

In Daily Life

For one whole week become an observer of your fears. Go about your normal daily life, but take note of the times when fearful thoughts or actions arise. As soon as possible after fear has been seen to arise, take some paper or a notebook and begin to reflect on what happened. Ask yourself the following questions:

- What preceded the fear?
- What situation or thought triggered it?
- How did it arise?
- What were the feelings immediately before it arose? Write it all down. Then, when you are ready, observe:
- How did you feel during the experience?
- Were there any other emotions present at the same time?
- Did you feel like you wanted to run away?
- Were you restless or rigid?
- Were you scared or calm?
- Were you hot or cold?
- Were you resisting it or accepting it?
- Did you experience physical sensations anywhere in your body during the fear or afterwards?

When you are ready, observe how you felt after the fear had gone:

- How long did the fear last?
- What sensations were there after the fear passed?
- How did you feel about being fearful?
- Were you able to come back to a peaceful state?

Continue doing this every time fear arises for at least a week, and longer if needed. Notice if the fear changes the more you observe it, or if you change in your attitude towards it. Begin to see where it is arising from within you. Get closer to it. See if you can make friends with it, even embrace it. Fear loses its power as you become more aware.

In Meditation

Find a quiet place to sit. Keep your back straight. Close your eyes and begin to watch your breath. Let your mind quieten as you flow with the rhythm of your breathing.

Now begin to watch your thoughts. Allow any thought to come up in your mind and let it go. Create a fearful thought and watch it enter – simply observe it. Breathe into it and maintain an attitude of being a witness. Keep doing this. The more you are able to observe, maintain the witness and not get involved with the thought, the more you will see clearly where the fear comes from.

As fear is seen to arise, watch what happens. In particular, observe what precedes the fear.

- Notice what triggers it to arise.
- Observe how you feel during the experience: whether you feel hot or cold, restless or rigid, scared or calm, resisting or accepting.
- Are there other emotions present at the same time?
- Do you want to stop meditating?
- How long does the fear last?
- Do you experience physical sensations anywhere in your body during the fear or afterwards?
- Observe how you feel at all times, simply witnessing the process.
- Observe where the fear is coming from. Breathe into that place.

If fear arises, connect with your heart. Breathe into your heart and feel you are releasing the fear. With every breath see the fear being released. Visualize each fear as a different-coloured bird flying away. It may take a while – you have had many fears digging deep for so long that it takes time to release the power they have. Remember, it is when you embrace fear that it loses its power. Breathe into your heart and release the fear. Embrace it in the heart.

4

THE GIFT
OF
FORGIVENESS

When we have touched another with forgiveness
we no longer require anything in return.
STEPHEN LEVINE

A few years ago we were taking part in a conference on men's
issues in Colorado. Paul was describing the abuse he had received
as a child from his father. Amongst other things, on a number of
occasions he had been threatened with a shotgun. Listening to
Paul brought up so many memories of the abuse I had experienced
with my father. I remember it as vividly as if it were yesterday. One
time I had just walked in and found my stepmother scolding my
brother. She was shouting for our father to come. When he came
into the room he immediately started hitting me! I kept saying that
it wasn't me, that it was my brother she was complaining about, but
he wouldn't listen, he just kept on hitting me.

EDDIE

At the conference, Paul talked with resentment and bitterness
about how he felt he could never forgive his father. Then a
man in the audience stood up and responded with, 'If you
cannot forgive, you will not be able to dance.' Those words

stayed with us as we walked away. Debbie thought of the monsters she had experienced under her bed when she was a child and how they had stopped her from being able to get out of bed. The monsters within us hold our energy back so that we cannot give or receive with ease. When we have monsters lurking in our minds we are unable to move freely, therefore we cannot dance.

Our ability to forgive is intricately connected to our emotional healing. Forgiveness is honouring ourselves and our humanity. It is not only pardoning another for the injustice they have caused us, but it is also saying, 'I care enough about myself not to want to carry this abuse, or to allow it to keep disturbing me, any more.' Another meaning for the word 'remission' is a surrendering, a forgiving, a pardoning of sins. In forgiving we release the pain, and in releasing the pain we can find our healing. What freedom this brings!

However, it is obviously far easier to talk about forgiveness than it is to do it. The pain surrounding our issues does not just disappear overnight. There may be the need to release anger, fear and other feelings about the way we have been treated, as well as to build a stronger sense of ourselves, before forgiveness can become imaginable. If we have been hurt or abused we invariably lose our sense of self-worth and self-esteem; rebuilding our confidence is essential. We need to take time to soften and soothe the pain, to make friends with ourselves.

If the pain is locked away it will fester and grow, keeping us in a state of separation, alienated from ourselves and each other. When repressed rage and hatred are freed, then there is the space for forgiveness to grow. The lack of forgiveness has divided families, races and countries, caused wars and tremendous suffering.

While I was working in a nursing home, I saw many older people stubbornly clinging to past resentments, unable to release them, stuck in the pain of bitterness and rage. They did not want to forgive. Some had children who would not let go of something done so long ago that even now, with the parent dying, they could not heal their pain and come together. It was extraordinarily hard for them to even think about forgiveness – the resentment and anger were so solid.

THE HEART OF FORGIVENESS

To forgive is to remove the boundaries that keep us isolated from each other. This is no easy task, as these boundaries are carefully constructed and maintained over the years. They provide us with an identity, supporting the ego in its need for security and self-protection. Releasing these boundaries goes against the ego's essential nature of holding on tight and being focused only on self; it attacks the very foundations of the fortress the ego has so laboriously built. To say, 'Forgive me' or 'I forgive you' means the ego has to back down and make room for softness and humility – not something it is fond of doing! As Ken Wilber explains in *Grace and Grit:*

> The theory behind forgiveness is simple: . . . if we are going to insist on identifying with just the little self in here, then others are going to bruise it, insult it, injure it. The ego actively collects hurts and insults, even while resenting them, because without its bruises it would be, literally, nothing. The ego's first manoeuver in dealing with this resentment is to try to get others to confess to their faults. 'You hurt me, say you're sorry.' . . . What the ego doesn't try is forgiveness, because that would undermine its very existence. To forgive others for insults, real or imagined, is to weaken the boundary between self and other.

If we believe we are separate and disconnected, then our actions will be self-centred and self-motivated. Yet such selfishness rarely satisfies the inner yearning for union or for intimacy. When we forgive, then this union is possible, for in the moment of forgiveness there is a releasing of boundaries and of that which separates one from another. The walls come down.

68

To forgive is to give first – it is a gift to ourselves. When we forgive we are giving ourselves the freedom of release. This means going beyond the hold of the ego. Rather than being on a high horse, casting dark looks at those who have wronged us, it is the courage to get off the horse and take the wrongdoing by the hand.

Forgiveness enables us to understand an otherwise uncompromising situation. It is soothing and healing. We are not trying to be simplistic. There are many instances when it seems that a good slap could solve an argument! But we are here to raise our consciousness, to heal the wounds, not to create new ones. By focusing on the anger we invariably create more anger; by focusing on the heart, anger has a chance to release itself and be resolved. We all have the potential to be more compassionate. Forgiveness is learning how to be both compassionate and generous.

This is not the same as forgetting, which can mean ignoring and dismissing the depth of feeling involved, the need to understand what happened, and the real impact of the incident. Forgetting does not necessarily resolve; in not acknowledging the feelings they may get put on hold in some distant recess, only to re-emerge and cause more problems at a later time. Forgetting without forgiving tends to create denial rather than encourage healing.

Forgiveness involves a full acknowledgement of what happened and the effect on all involved. It is an acceptance of the pain that has been caused and, at the same time, a dropping of the charges against the accused. Once there is full acknowledgement then what is the benefit of continuing the pain? If the wrongdoing has been seen for what it is and the hurt feelings have been voiced, what do we gain by not forgiving?

The healing journey brings us to a place of confronting that which is holding us back from being able to forgive, and it is forgiveness that enables us to continue. If healing is wholeness, then to heal is to accept our whole being; this means the forgiveness of both ourselves and others, and the developing of a gentleness and sensitivity. Just as it is difficult to jump into the sea when we think the water is cold, and yet when we do it is so worth it, in the same way, when we take the plunge into the ocean of forgiveness it can be surprisingly refreshing and enjoyable!

One night in our therapy group one of the group leaders put her shopping bag in the middle of the room and said, 'This is my bitterness, guilt and hate that I have been carrying around. I feel lighter without it.' She walked away. But then she turned around and went back, saying, 'I actually feel more comfortable with it, so I think I will continue carrying it around even though it's heavy and weighs me down.' I went home and pondered over that one. Then I realised I didn't need my bitterness and hate any more. It had helped me to get through the past four years since my husband had left me, but now I could let go and even forgive him. I felt lighter not having to carry this burden of grief, hate and rejection any more. I phoned my ex-husband at work and told him that I forgave him. How I would have liked to be a fly on the wall when he took that call!

PAT ASMAN

FORGIVING OURSELVES

When we consider forgiveness we usually think in terms of our forgiving someone else: that this other person (or persons) has done something to me and I am therefore in a position to forgive them, or not, as the case may be. In this scenario, we are the abused, hurt or shamed party and the other is the one who has done the act of wrongdoing.

Conversely, there is the opposite situation where we are in a position of asking for forgiveness from someone whom we have hurt or wronged. This means having to be humble. Our ability to be at peace with what has happened will depend upon being forgiven by this other person. If they do not forgive, then the situation stays with us, often creating guilt or fear. Asking for forgiveness is discussed further on in this chapter.

For there is a third place where forgiveness is needed, and it is, in many ways, the most important place. And that is the forgiveness of ourselves. It is by far the hardest place to start.

70

As Treya so honestly shared in Ken Wilber's book *Grace and Grit*:

> Forgiving means accepting myself. Gulp! This means giving up an old friend of mine – self-criticism. My scorpion companion. When I visualise all the things that prevent me from feeling right about myself, then, up higher than the rest, as a kind of backdrop to all my other 'problems' is a figure of a scorpion with its tail arched over its back. On the verge of stinging itself. This is my self-criticism, cutting myself down relentlessly, feeling unlovable, the background feeling behind all the other problems, the grievances against myself that keep me from seeing the light and the miracles that can only be seen in that light. Hmmm. The big one.

There are a number of reasons for starting with ourselves. Firstly, if we are the wronged party then there can be a very deep insecurity within us that says, 'Well, if this is what happened, then somewhere along the line I must have done something to deserve this', or words to that effect. If the abuse occurred when we were children, this is a very natural thought pattern.

To a child, parents are God, authority, the highest on this earth, the most important thing in life. If mother or father is being abusive, then it couldn't possibly be something wrong in them so the problem must be in me, the child. I must have done something to deserve this.

If the wrongdoing occurred not in childhood but later in life, and with someone other than parents, then it still touches our deepest place of insecurity. Even as adults, and even when we know that the wrongdoing has nothing to do with us personally and it is, rather, an expression of the other person's own pain, there is still an underlying feeling of blaming ourselves in some way: we were in the wrong place, we should have known better, we must have been giving out the wrong messages, we must have done something to deserve it, and so on. This self-blame hinders our healing and holds us in a state of confusion and hopelessness.

I grew up in a family of nine children. I was never happy, always feeling dirty, ashamed, guilty, even when I was dressed I felt naked. I clung to everyone I could, searching for love. Slowly I realised that every time I went in search of love I would be sexually abused. I married at twenty years old. My husband was an abusive man, abusing me sexually, drinking a lot, then causing me further torture (if he couldn't sleep then I wasn't allowed to). My worst experience was of my husband raping me while I was in bed with our two little girls. I found it hard to forgive myself for not being strong enough to protect my children, but it was easier to play dead than to fight back.

After thirty years of marriage and six children I began to question myself. With the help of a therapist I started an inward and often painful journey. I remembered being sexually abused from before the age of two years and how, as time went on, I learned to switch off from my body so as to cope with the pain. As my journey progressed I got the courage to take control of my life. How to say 'no' to being a victim. I ended my marriage. Somehow I have forgiven my husband and my father. I feel such freedom! The most difficult part has been in forgiving myself, but I feel I am there. From being a stranger to myself, I am now my own best friend. I thought I deserved everything bad that happened to me, today I know I deserve the best!

BRIDGET

Secondly, there is the pain we may have brought to others and the need to forgive ourselves for having done this. We often ask at workshops how many people feel free of personal guilt, have forgiven themselves for past deeds that may have caused hurt to someone else. There are usually only a few people who answer in the affirmative. Guilt tends to stay with us, to hold us in fear of ourselves, to keep us from being free: I am such a bad person! How could I have done such a thing? What happens if I do it again? How can I ever trust myself? How can I ever be trusted? This is the nature of guilt – unrepentant and repetitive!

When we visited Margaret, in Scotland, she told us how, two years previously, she had been looking after her daughter's puppy when it fell ill and eventually died. Deep inside,

Margaret was convinced it was her fault that the dog had died, that in some way she had not cared for it enough, had not done all that she could have to help. For two years she had carried this guilt, never telling anyone and unable to forgive herself. She cried when she finally told us. The sadness was the fact that she disliked herself so much. It is easy to find things we do not like about ourselves. How much more liberating to forgive ourselves and let the drama go!

My father and I had always been close, seeing each other daily even after I left home. In my early fifties I became interested in yoga and decided to go to a yoga centre for two weeks to have a chance to really learn – it was the first time I had been away on my own without family or parents! While I was there, my father fell seriously ill. I got to his bedside just a few hours before he died. Now it is six years later, and I still feel guilty for having been away for those last two weeks of his life. I have never rejoiced that I was there for the last few hours and was able to say 'I love you' before he died. I just feel this great burden of guilt. I know that this guilt has stopped me from being able to celebrate my father's life.

PETER JEFFRIES

You may remember Mary, whom we spoke of in Chapter 1. She was still feeling deeply guilty for not having been present when her husband died some four years previously. As Mary worked with forgiveness, she began consciously to accept that her husband was not holding it against her, and that she could make peace in her mind and release the guilt. She had believed the guilt was her atonement. When she saw how it was actually creating further suffering, and that she was doing this to herself, it became clear that she was ready to release it. She had been punishing herself for something that could never be changed, could never be redeemed. She was then able to turn it around and see that she could honour the memory of her husband more by making her life a worthy one. The joy on her face that day was delightful! The two practices later in this chapter offer specific ways of working with guilt and forgiveness.

We begin to develop forgiveness for ourselves when we see that who we were when we committed the act for which we still feel so guilty is not who we are now. By no means is this a way of brushing off the importance or magnitude of what we may have done – rather it is seeing ourselves more objectively. For no matter if the deed was as close as yesterday, or as far away as fifty years ago, we are no longer the same person. We have already changed our feelings, our understanding of life and the way we behave. Every cell in our body changes every seven years. From one day to the next we are not the same person, physically, mentally or emotionally.

Who you have been is someone you can observe, as if you are looking at another person. Can you see the fear, confusion, anger and conflict from which you reacted? Can you see the pain you were feeling inside that made you lash out and cause further pain? Can you feel compassion for this person that you were? Can you open your heart to forgiving this person, holding yourself in your arms, gently, lovingly? You may want to take some time to yourself to consider this, to be with who you were and who you are now.

Accepting what we did does not make the deed permissible. We do not have to accept the act, but we can forgive ourselves; seeing the ignorance and confusion from which we acted, we can forgive and release. Taking a deep breath, letting life move on, letting go of the past and opening our arms to the present. Accepting our mistakes we release them with compassion, release the guilt within so we can breathe more deeply. We embrace who we really are, recognizing our understanding, tenderness and generosity. Jeremy Hayward, in a lecture at Naropa Institute in Colorado, reminds us: 'We need to let go of guilt, let go of sin, let go of blame, let go of thinking that we made a mistake; stop looking for the problems that have to be corrected, rather than the goodness and intelligence that can be nourished.'

We may also have a deep regret for how we have lived. Few of us, even with successful careers or ideal families, actually feel complete and at peace. Instead there can be an underlying dissatisfaction, a sense of feeling lost, incomplete, a guilt at somehow not finding the fulfilment we were meant to find, or at having made too many mistakes. There may be an unexplainable grief that is, at times, overwhelming. Releasing this grief is an essential part of the healing process. In the releasing and forgiving we can find a deeper place of contentment. John Bradshaw says how: 'Until we learn to forgive we cannot finish the past, and until we finish with the past we cannot be complete adult human beings in the present.'

TIME OUT: To Look at Guilt

Have some paper and a pen with you. Take a few minutes to settle, watching your breath as it enters and leaves your body. You are becoming quieter. Then gently bring to mind any guilt you have been or are feeling about a past issue or issues. When you are ready, ask yourself these questions. Let the answers come in their own way. You might want to do some writing in a notebook to go deeper into the implications touched on here. Try taking each of the questions and, starting a new page, allow yourself to write freely and honestly. Don't forget to breathe!

- Is feeling this guilt actually helping me in some way?
- Does it makes me feel better?
- Am I finding redemption through my guilt?
- Do I feel that my suffering now balances the suffering I caused?
- Do I feel that I have no right to be forgiven?
- If so, why?
- Does the thought of being free of guilt feel wrong?
- Am I still the same person I was when the situation took place that triggered this guilt?
- How have I changed since that time?
- If I am not the same person, then can I forgive the person who I was?
- Can I recognize my weaknesses without feeling guilty?
- Can I take full responsibility for what happened and let it go?

- If not, what is holding me back?

Ask any other questions that arise. For healing to deepen, it is essential that you get clear on your real feelings. Working with guilt and forgiveness can take some time. Forgiveness is the tenderness and warmth we can offer ourselves that is so vital to healing.

FORGIVING OTHERS

From bringing ourselves into our heart and experiencing how forgiveness is so essential for healing, we can now take a deep breath and begin to direct our forgiveness to others. Most important is the willingness to start, the willingness to embrace the movement from a place of hurt and pain to a place of healing and wholeness.

It is important to connect with the depth of our feelings: I feel hurt / angry / you did this to me / no birthday present / adultery / you raped me / never being there / no support / you made my life a living hell. And, in finding that place, to enter fearlessly. In so doing, anything may arise: anger, resentment, bitterness. Fury at how we were treated, the wrongs done against us, the injustices and the hurt.

For instance, if we have previously chosen not to deal with the feelings surrounding the loss of a loved one, but have instead ignored the remorse, abandonment and even anger, we may now find ourselves confronting these feelings. Or perhaps we are maintaining an injurious relationship while waiting for the day when eventually we will be loved, acknowledged or desired. For that longed-for moment when a parent expresses their caring rather than their dismissal, when an abusive partner turns into our lover. It is essential to bring these feelings into our conscious mind, to know how powerful they are and the debilitating effect they can have upon us.

It is not always easy to forgive. Having been insulted, betrayed, disrespected or misused, we may now wonder how we

76

can forgive unless there is retribution of some kind, some recognition of the pain caused. We have been violated and it feels terrible. We want to strike back, get even, be revenged. But does this heal? Does revenge bring completion and release? Or does it maintain separateness, rejection and hatred?

Taking revenge may seem like a clear statement about the wrong done to us and our hurt feelings, but in reality we are the ones who are suffering the most. The hurt feelings are a burden; they weigh us down and limit our movement. They emotionally bind us so that we cannot be free – always we are this person who was hurt or rejected. We are hurting due to someone else's actions, yet in maintaining the resentment and bitterness we are feeling even more pain. So often people say that they can never forgive, and we do understand the enormous agony that could make someone feel this way. But is it worth destroying life for? Without forgiveness there will always be hatred, anger and pain.

And no matter how long we continue feeling bitter and hurt, it can never change what happened. Our mother did not treat us kindly, our lover did not love us in return, our child was killed. The act is done, that is the reality. The more important issue is to find our healing in the midst of such resentment or anger. For the only place where real change can occur is within ourselves, in our heart, in the gentleness of our own embrace. Forgiveness could be the greatest gift we will ever give ourselves.

I had been working on my relationship with my father for so long. I had been in therapy since I was eighteen, had gone through layer upon layer of rejection issues, need issues, security issues, confronting him, talking to him, working with myself, forgiving him, then not forgiving him. And then, finally, in my late thirties, I came to a point where I didn't want to be abused any more. It was that simple. I just didn't want it any more. I knew that I had been maintaining my relationship with him in the vague hope that some day he would change. That he would actually be able to say something nice, something affirming or loving. I didn't expect him to be able to say 'I love you', but just something positive, some form of acknowledgement. I was waiting and waiting for this day to

come and in the meantime I was allowing myself to be emotionally
abused.

And then I found a place where I did not need that love or
affirmation from him. I was connecting with such a deep accept-
ance of myself that I no longer needed it from him, it didn't matter
any more. The need had gone. And as I released my need for him I
also released my inability to forgive him. Now I was able to see the
hurt and confused man that he really was, the wounded child who
had no idea how to love. I saw how his pain was far greater than
mine, how he had no real connection to his heart. I had been too
locked into my own pain to have seen this before.

D.H.

That story illustrates how difficult it is to separate our feelings
from someone who is hurting or abusing us, to be able to see
this other person clearly for who they are. Engrossed in our
own pain and anger there is no space in us to realize how the
abuser is being so deeply driven by their own pain. It is easy to
say, 'Why should I care?', but it is when we care that we connect
with our own healing.

When we are really at peace, at ease and joyful within
ourselves, it is not possible for us to hurt anyone else – we can
barely even hurt a fly! When we respect ourselves, we respect
all life; when we open our own heart, we enter into the hearts
of all others. To inflict pain or abuse on someone else means
that the pain being felt inside ourselves is so great that it has to
find some form of escape, some way to be released.So when we
are hurting we invariably end up hurting another. The pain
within the abuser is often far greater than the pain being
imposed on the abused.

If we can separate our own pain from that which is the pain
in the person hurting us, it can help us to forgive. There is our
own distress that arises naturally in response to being hurt, and
there is the distress that we have received but is actually what
the abuser is feeling. We can give back that which does not
belong to us. This creates a space between ourselves and the
one hurting us. In this space lies our forgiveness. Then we can
see this other person for who they really are, with their own
hopelessness and confusion. Yes, we got hurt! But it is also

possible to forgive, to have compassion. In *Seeking the Heart of Wisdom*, J. Goldstein and J. Kornfield point out how:

> When we feel anger towards someone, we can consider that he or she is a being just like us, who has faced much suffering in life. If we had experienced the same circumstances and history of suffering as the other person, might we not act in the same way? So we allow ourselves to feel compassion, to feel his or her suffering.

We can know this through our own experience. Remembering those times we have hurt someone, we can see the anger and conflict we were feeling at the time. And although it may not have felt good to lash out, there was also a sense of release. We hurt others most when we are hurting. If we know this in ourselves, then can we not know it in someone else? Can we not see how great another's pain is? Can we not see how an abusive parent is also a wounded child? How a rejecting lover may also have been rejected?

Let us be clear that forgiveness is not necessarily about forgiving the act (i.e. abuse) but about forgiving the actor (i.e. abuser). We know the act for what it is; that it is atrocious, painful, irreconcilable or unacceptable. We acknowledge this and can state clearly that there is no acceptance of the act. Forgiveness is concerned with the person behind the act and in coming to some understanding of this person. We don't have to forgive the act, but we can forgive the person and hope they will change. This helps release the pain we are feeling about what took place. Holding on to the lack of forgiveness keeps our own pain alive.

I was sitting in the meditation hall when Swami Satchidananda, an Indian holy man, started talking about Adolf Hitler, the holocaust and the horrendous treatment of the Jews. It is a tender subject that can easily offend. I felt squeamish because here we were sitting in the most peaceful atmosphere and one of the most unpeaceful subjects was being addressed. I listened attentively as he said, 'We even need to forgive Adolf Hitler.'

My immediate reaction was horror. 'Why? How? What about the millions who suffered?'

This was a subject that I as a Jew never thought I would confront. Hitler was the last person I wanted to forgive! However, I saw that while I was experiencing the hate, feeling it throughout my being, Hitler wasn't feeling it. That as long as we hate Hitler, he is still committing crimes against humanity, through our pain. And he isn't even alive! With hate inside me I could not be free. I thought if I could forgive Hitler, I could forgive anyone. The acts he committed were infinitely terrible and I could never condone them, but the person who did those acts was acting from complete ignorance. His mind was disturbed in the worst possible way, a madman beyond belief. How could anyone in their right mind come anywhere near committing such atrocities? He was sick.

But since we are all connected, in essence, I can only have compassion. In this way I am not adding to the hate or the atrocity. By my compassion I help lessen the pain in the world. So I swallowed hard, followed with a deep sigh and some conscious breathing, and wondered if I could learn to keep forgiving and forgiving and forgiving.

EDDIE

To forgive others is to recognize those hearts that are not yet open. To see how the inner pain is keeping the heart closed and locked in, so there is no free movement. Forgiving is not condoning the act, therefore it does not imply that a murderer should not go to prison or be rehabilitated in some way. It is recognizing that, due to our ignorance, we create pain. When we forget our essential interconnectedness and the humanness that we share, then we hurt each other, not understanding that at the same time we are also hurting ourselves. There is a greater purpose for us in being here. It is not just to get caught up in dramas and confusions, but to contribute to the sanity and beauty of this world.

ASKING FOR FORGIVENESS

Equally as important as being able to forgive another is the courage to ask for forgiveness from someone we may have hurt. This is a tender subject. We usually only hurt another when we are in an agitated, defensive or insecure place. We are feeling vulnerable and lash out. Now we are recognizing what we did and want to heal, but it takes tremendous courage. To take our pride in our hands and admit we were wrong and to ask to be forgiven – for this great humility is needed.

To ask for forgiveness is therefore an act of the fearless warrior. At first there may be much resistance – a battle with our ego. How hard it is to admit we were wrong! And even if we can admit it to ourselves, dare we expose such failings and weaknesses to another? Will we be granted clemency or rejected even further? In *The Caring Question* Donald and Nancy Tubesing suggest:

> The starting point is to acknowledge that forgiveness is not a feeling, it's a choice. It's actually two choices – the decision made by one person to repent, and the decision made by the other to forgive. When you've done something in which you need forgiveness, admit it. Swallow your pride, take the risk, and make your request directly to the injured person: 'Will you forgive me? I really hurt you, and I'm sorry.' This kind of direct request gives the other person the chance to say, 'Yes, I forgive you,' rather than retaliate.

Asking for forgiveness creates a vulnerable and open place. We are not only recognizing the pain we have caused, but also acknowledging our role in that pain. It lets the other person know that we do care, that we are a friend. This is so important. That we are not so arrogant we cannot take responsibility for what we have done or admit to the effect of our actions. When pain is acknowledged, it takes the heat out and cools the air. We may not be forgiven immediately, but the door is now open – there is the space for each person to find their healing.

We can ask for forgiveness even if we think we are right. Because as long as we have hurt another, then being right does not necessarily matter as much as bringing peace and comfort and thereby healing the whole situation. It is glorious to see the smile of forgiveness on another's face. How healing that can be! Sometimes the other person will not understand, but by asking for forgiveness it gives them a chance to look at themselves and their own participation in the situation.

And at times a peace offering, such as a bunch of flowers, is a way of showing our genuine concern and love. We recently had a miscommunication with our seventy-three-year-old neighbour. Later we brought him some flowers. His face lit up as he smelt their sweet fragrance!

There may also be times when actually to ask for forgiveness from someone else is not appropriate. If we are experiencing unresolved issues with someone who has died and we want to release the pain, or if we are experiencing negative communication with someone and are not in a position to talk with them about it, then we can work with ourselves. There may be an unconscious participation in the conflict, and if this is released even on just one side, then both sides have a chance to heal. The practice at the end of this chapter is the one referred to in the following story illustrating this point:

> *I was directing an educational institute and one of the main teachers really had it in for me. I knew that it was issues to do with power and control and jealousy, but she was turning people against me and pushing me into a corner. It wasn't easy to deal with! So I brought her into my meditation, asking her for forgiveness for whatever I might have done to her, and forgiving her for what she was doing to me. I did this every day. After a few days I noticed she was letting up a bit. By the end of a week she had virtually stopped. Another week and it was over. I don't think she was aware of the change in herself at all. I realized that through the forgiveness meditation I had released whatever hook I had in me and so she had nowhere to hang her projection. It was amazing to watch it happen.*

DEBBIE

It is vital to recognize that all that has happened to us, whether we were abused or rejected, whatever pain we have personally experienced or are still experiencing, is not the whole of us. The 'abused me' is not our entire being, only one part. Being so powerful, awful or shameful, this part can be overwhelming. But it is only a part, and inside we are many other things too. There is a unique us that is free and alive. We can hold the hurt part of ourselves with love, embracing it, seeing it for what it is. But we can also recognize the rest of our being, that which is caring and loving and joyful.

When we forgive, all the energy that was being used to maintain the guilt, shame, anger or resentment is released. As if a dam were bursting, we are flooded with warmth and an abundant freedom. We can breathe! We can dance! Forgiveness creates the space for movement; it is being bold and heroic. Let us be committed to our healing in every moment and every day. A commitment that is real, genuine, and comes from our heart. When we get caught up in things, let us be forgiving of ourselves. When we get entangled with others, let us forgive them. Let us not shame ourselves or others. Then we can dance together!

So when the shoe fits
The foot is forgotten,
When the belt fits
The belly is forgotten,
When the heart is right
'For' and 'against' are forgotten.
THOMAS MERTON

PRACTICE – Forgiveness Meditation

Allow at least thirty minutes for this practice. Have some paper and a pen with you. Find a quiet place and make yourself comfortable, whether sitting on a cushion on the floor, or in a chair. Take a deep breath and release it.

Spend a few minutes watching the breath as it enters and leaves the body. As you watch the flow of the breath, feel yourself relaxing. With each out breath feel any tension or stress leaving. With every in breath feel quietness and openness growing and expanding in you.

Silently repeat, 'I am relaxing.'

Now bring your attention to the area of your heart. Breathe into that area. Relax and soften the heart. Then bring an image or thought of yourself as you are into that area. Visualize and hold yourself there, with gentleness. As you do so, become aware of forgiveness, open yourself to forgiving yourself.

Silently and slowly repeat the words, 'I forgive myself. I forgive myself. I forgive myself. For any harm I have done, knowingly or unknowingly, whether through thought, through words or through actions, I forgive myself.'

Keep repeating these words. As you do this, all sorts of resistances may arise – all the reasons why you should not be forgiven, all the things you have done that are unworthy, and all the shameful or guilty feelings associated with these things. Breathe into these resistances, acknowledge them, and then let them go. Whatever arises is OK, but do not get involved. It is important to continue with the practice, with repeating the words and generating forgiveness. Release the resistances with your out breath. Come back to the heart with your in breath.

Let the forgiveness fill your entire being. Hold yourself in your heart as a mother would hold her child, tenderly, gently, with complete forgiveness. Know that you are forgiven. Feel the forgiveness wash through your whole being. 'I am forgiven. I am forgiven. I am forgiven.'

Now bring into your heart someone who needs to be forgiven by you, or someone you would like to forgive. Hold this person in your heart. Feel their presence. Breathe into any feelings that arise, breathing out any resistances, anger, pain or fear. Soften the belly, breathe into your heart.

Silently say to this person, 'I forgive you. I forgive you. I forgive you. I forgive you for the harm you have inflicted, knowingly or unknowingly, through your thoughts, through your words or by your actions. I forgive you.'

Breathe into any resistances that may arise. At first it may be difficult to forgive, but every step is a step towards healing. Take your time, keep repeating the words. See what it is that is holding you back, and let it go on each out breath. As you forgive, the boundaries between the two of you begin to dissolve. Hold this person in your heart and feel your forgiveness embracing them, loving them. Embrace each other in your heart. Silently repeat, 'I forgive you.'

Now bring into your heart someone from whom you wish to ask for forgiveness, someone whom you may have wronged or who has therefore closed their heart to you. Bring this person into your heart and hold them there with your love and forgiveness.

Silently repeat the words, 'I ask for your forgiveness. I ask for your forgiveness. I ask for your forgiveness. If I have hurt or harmed you, knowingly or unknowingly, through my thoughts, through my words or through my actions, please forgive me.'

Breathe into any resistance you may feel coming from the other person, breathe into the resentment, the hurt, the pain. Accept your own vulnerability. Keep repeating the words. As the forgiveness grows, let their forgiveness pour through you. Feel your hearts opening to each other, embracing each other. Know that you are forgiven, that the forgiveness is in your heart. Allow yourself to be forgiven.

Now come back to yourself in your heart. Feel the joy of forgiveness in every part of your being. You are forgiven. You have forgiven. You have been forgiven. Let the release and the gratitude pour through you. Let the love that is within you radiate throughout your entire being.

This practice may take time to develop. If you keep doing it, you will see the benefits. You are on your way to healing. Rejoice in the forgiveness!

5

BODYMIND
WISDOM

As a man thinketh, so will he be.
BIBLE

In the Buddhist tradition, to be born as a human being is to be
born with the greatest possible conditions for self-realization,
for healing into our greater potential. The human body is
considered to be the most precious of all forms as it is the
vehicle through which we can embody our true freedom.
There is a wonderful Tibetan story about a blind turtle that
lives in the ocean and comes to the surface only once every
thousand years. A gold ring floats in the ocean. The Tibetans
say that the chance the blind turtle will put its head into that
ring when it comes up for air is as rare as it is for a human to
take birth, therefore making each life extremely precious. This
preciousness of life is also seen in the Hindu tradition, where it
is considered necessary to take birth in the human form in
order to be liberated from the cycle of birth and rebirth. It is
said that only by having a human body is it possible to transcend all limited states of existence.

Yet there are other spiritual and religious traditions where the body is not so well favoured. Indeed, in some it is considered to be an obstacle, a hindrance, something that gets in the way of spiritual growth, holding back such development through the distraction of physical pain, the need to fulfil bodily functions or satisfy bodily requirements. Occasionally, as the body is so disregarded, it is even used to create more pain through flagellation or extreme austerity, thereby proving the power of the mind over the weakness of the flesh.

In the West we too worship the body, but more as an object of desire than as a vehicle for liberation. We make sure it is given the right nourishment and is well exercised, although this is to improve appearances or for health, rather than to better the conditions for spiritual development. Even though we may not regard our physical form as an obstacle or hindrance, nor feel the need to practise austerity, none the less we may feel quite separate from the inner workings or energies flowing through us. The emphasis is on the external image, not on an internal relationship. So despite living inside this body for many years, when it goes wrong it can feel as if we are inside a complete stranger. We tend to view illness or disease as something coming from outside, something alien that takes us over. When we get ill we search for someone to make us right again, rather than looking within ourselves.

In the East, there is a different approach to the body, based on an understanding of the energy – known as Chi – that flows throughout our entire being. Complex systems have developed over a period of five thousand years that map these energy flows and how to key into them. The healthy balance of these energies maintains our entire physical system. Illness is therefore seen as a result of blockages in the flow, and balance is sought by releasing these blockages and freeing the energy needed for healing. As we all should, naturally, be in a state of wellness, when someone becomes ill the question asked is why this person is not healthy – what causes are detrimentally influencing them. Every aspect of their life is taken into account, not just the physical ones. In approaching illness from this standpoint, a deeper understanding of the relationship between the person, their life and the illness is reached. Any

87

difficulties are not seen as just coming from outside the body, but as an intricate part of the whole.

Which brings us to another way of relating to the body, and that is to see it as a part of ourselves, an extension of our inner being expressing itself physically. Here we discover an intricate relationship existing between all the different aspects – the psychological, emotional and the physical; they are a flow of energies in constant communication. Just as each individual cannot exist independently but is dependent on, and exists in relationship to, all other things, in the same way the body and mind are not independent entities but exist in relationship with each other, each influencing and affecting the whole. The many experiences we have, emotional difficulties or long-held thoughts or beliefs, feelings about ourselves, the stress and tension in our lives – all are registered in and affect the physical body as much as they do the mind. Like a plane's black box, our bodies record our every experience. It is as if, in Stephen Levine's words, 'the body is just solidified mind', or, as Reshad Field says in *Here to Heal*: 'What we put out in thought will always come back and land in the same area where we tightened at that moment.'

In perceiving the intimate relationship between the mind and the body, it becomes clear that if we leave out any one part of the picture then wholeness is not possible. If we focus only on the physical and not the psychological or emotional, then we limit our healing potential. With this understanding, illnesses or physical difficulties become something to connect with, perhaps even to make friends with, for they are a part of our whole being. There is no need to feel powerless or in the grip of something beyond our control. All the various changes and expressions within the body are teachers, and invaluable insight can be gained when we learn to listen and pay attention, when we see our body as a friend and not as an enemy, when we can love it and not despise or reject it. As we get to know our body more intimately, we are able to participate more fully in the healing process. The two practices later in this chapter will help you get to know your body and understand the language being used.

In this context, rather than exploring the many possible cures for physical symptoms, the purpose is to deepen our understanding of ourselves. Where a cure may be dependent upon different external factors, such as medication or surgery, healing is done within ourselves, by ourselves. In *Chop Wood Carry Water*, Rick Fields says: 'Healing is a basic human function; not a medical touch or a supernatural power.' By entering into an exploration of the body, the effect of the mind on the body, and the flow of energy between all the various parts of ourselves, we can awaken that function.

THE BODYMIND RELATIONSHIP

The greatest force in the human body is the natural drive of the body to heal itself – but that force is not independent of the belief system, which can translate expectations into physiological change. Nothing is more wondrous about the fifteen billion neurons in the human brain than their ability to convert thoughts, hopes, ideas, and attitudes into chemical substances. Everything begins, therefore, with belief. What we believe is the most powerful option of all.

NORMAN COUSINS

The medical world is well aware of how fear can create nausea and, if prolonged, may result in a stomach ulcer; how constipation, accidents or catching a virus become more common during stressful situations such as moving house, getting married or starting a new job. The conflicts and uncertainties at such times can leave us feeling vulnerable, out of balance, 'out of sorts'. Perhaps we need to take time off, to have a 'mental health' day. Such recuperation time gives us a chance to accept the new situation and to realign to the changes. It is also known how sadness or depression can make us feel very low in energy – we tend to put on weight and to catch colds or get headaches. Conversely, when we are feeling joyful or elated we feel physically full of energy, with less need for sleep; there is a greater resistance to illness and our body tends to be healthier, more vibrant. Feeling good is good for the immune system!

These are simple examples of a far more complex relationship, of an intricate network constantly communicating between all the millions of cells throughout our entire psychological and physical being. What we are feeling in one area is also felt in all others, and what we are not expressing in one area may therefore find expression in another. Imagine a tube of toothpaste with the top firmly screwed on; now imagine that you are trying to squeeze some of the toothpaste out of the tube, but have forgotten to take the top off! What happens? The toothpaste will find another way out, usually by coming out of the bottom of the tube. In the same way, when we are stressed but do not take time to relate to it, to acknowledge what is happening and to relax and ease the tension, the stress will find another form of expression. It will get pushed down into the body and physical difficulties may develop.

As we think so we become; therefore, as we have become, so we can see how we have been thinking. However, it is not the conscious thoughts and feelings that are influencing the body, for we are aware of these. Rather it is the unconscious – the prejudices, resentments, insecurities, fears and worries – that we are not consciously aware of. These find their expression through the body. Understanding the bodymind language is therefore a way of seeing into the hidden parts, the areas of our being that have become repetitious and habitual, memories locked away and ignored, attitudes that are ingrained. All can be found reflected in the body, influencing our health and well-being.

I had a lot of decisions to make about various aspects of my life. My tendency is to avoid making a decision and allow things to happen naturally. This may be fine with me but where other people are concerned it tends to create a confusing environment. When they are not dealt with, problems have a habit of piling up on themselves until everyone becomes alienated. Not knowing which way to turn, I began to get fearful and lost touch with myself. I did not want to face up to the reality of what was happening and was judging myself to be a failure. An incident with my parents reminded me of similar incidents from when I was a child that had left me feeling alienated and unloved. I couldn't face any of it — the past, the difficulties, my fears, the responsibilities. And then the pain began — acute sinusitis — in my face and head, the very place I was wanting to turn away from.

HELEN HUMPHRIES

We influence our well-being through the inner messages that we convey to the body. As Shakespeare said, 'Cheerfulness is health; the opposite, melancholy, is disease.' If the message we are giving the body is one of irritation or annoyance with ourselves, self-dislike or depression, the body will respond with a low energy level, lack of vitality, muscle ache or indigestion. When negative or destructive thought patterns – such as worry, guilt, anger, self-criticism or fear – are maintained over a long period of time they begin to affect us on ever deeper levels. After all, if someone kept calling you ugly, wouldn't you start to feel bad? And doesn't it feel better when someone calls you beautiful or handsome?

When we give the body messages of acceptance, forgiveness, love, enjoyment and appreciation, it will respond accordingly with brightness, vibrancy and good health. Bernie Siegel writes in his book *Love, Medicine and Miracles* of how contentment used to be considered a prerequisite for health. Yet how many of us are really content?

Agnes came over to talk to me. We were sitting on the floor together and she was telling me about the arthritis in her joints, especially in her feet. As she talked she kept criticizing herself, saying how she knew she should be massaging her feet but never seemed to find the time, how she kept meaning to do specific yoga postures but she was not very good at them, how she had changed her diet but was such a bad cook that she didn't think it was helping. After a while I gently mentioned to her that arthritis was sometimes associated with an over-critical personality. Agnes fell backwards as if she had been hit over the head! Criticism, especially self-criticism, was her biggest issue. We talked about her focusing on acceptance and forgiveness, about highlighting what was right rather than what was wrong, about having some compassion and love for herself.

91

After a while she said, 'I have a feeling that if I can let go of the criticism, then maybe I can begin to heal the arthritis.'

DEBBIE

In exploring the bodymind relationship, it is not intended to oversimplify the concept of the mind affecting the body. It is not that we cause our illnesses, nor are we to blame if we are ill. Firstly, there are far too many factors involved in the making of our whole being to say that only one thing is the cause – there are numerous external and environmental factors as well as internal influences. Secondly, to say that we create our own reality does not allow for any other force in our lives than ourselves. This is too extreme and self-centred, especially when we consider the interconnectedness of all things. We are too intimately involved and related to each other to be the only controlling factor in our reality. We are a part of reality, not the cause of it.

Although we do not create our own reality, we do affect how we react to what happens to us. We can react or we can respond. We can choose to sink into illness, pain or crisis; or we can choose to use the situation to release resentments, practise forgiveness, develop compassion and find healing. In so doing we enter into a world of greater understanding.

Physical difficulties can teach us great lessons. By paying attention to our feelings when we enter into a pained part of the body, by really listening to what that part of the body is trying to tell us, we will hear the messages. What we are unable to recognize in the mind may become clear through the body. Areas where we are holding tight can be relaxed, the tension released, so we enter into the core of the issue. Illness can be a great life-saver, a turning point, an opportunity to look within and make changes. It is a chance to see what is important, what is missing, and to create a new space in which to live.

In my teens and early twenties I was searching for a spiritual path. Then I got caught up in the joys of the body and forgot spirituality. But as the years went by I was feeling increasingly alienated, emotionally dried up and unable to love. I was divorced. My life seemed to revolve around the meaningless struggle of corporate success. I was certainly climbing a ladder in business terms, but I was not happy deep inside. There was an emptiness, a longing. One day I was mending the roof of my house and as I stepped on to the ladder to come down, it slipped. I fell to the ground, smashing my pelvis into many pieces.

Lying flat on my back for three months gave me tremendous time for reflection. My body wasted away but my heart had a chance to be heard. Everything had to change. I realized how desperately lost I had been, trying to fill the emptiness through work; how loveless my life had become. The hardest change was going from being a long-distance runner to being barely able to walk. Until I saw that I simply had to find a new direction, new ground to walk on, in particular to reconnect with that original longing for the sacred and spiritual and to bring it into my daily life. I went from climbing the corporate ladder to falling off it and finding fulfilment in joining a healing circle! Now I am so glad the accident happened – it enabled me to start a new life.

F.W.

TIME OUT: To Understand the Bodymind Language

Do this practice lying down. Use a pillow beneath your head and a blanket to cover you. Have some paper and a pen near you. Eyes are closed, arms by your side, palms upward, feet slightly apart. Take a few minutes to relax, watching your breath coming in and out of your body. Become one with the breath, letting your thoughts quieten and your body sink into the floor.

When you are ready, begin to focus on the part of your body that is ill or in pain. Bring your mind to that part of you. Relax into it. Begin to explore all the various aspects of this area: the colours, shape, texture, whether it is soft or hard, how big it is, how it feels. Spend as much time as you want in exploring all the different aspects of this part of your being.

Now, if you can, go back to the time before you had this difficulty. In your mind remember how your body was,

93

and then how it began to change. Take your time.

When you have done so, see if you can expand this memory to what was happening in your life during the year before your illness. Slowly follow through that year. Allow it to fill your mind. See if any clues or messages come through to you from this period of time. See if you can make a connection between what was happening then and your physical condition.

Then bring your mind back to your body as it is now. See how your illness is affecting your life, your relationships, your feelings about yourself, your work, your attitude towards being alive. Focus on the effect of your illness.

Now, gently, ask your illness if there is anything it would like to tell you. Let it speak in its own time and in its own way. Ask it what it needs from you, and how you can help it to heal.

When you are ready, become aware of the room around you. Turn over on your side and write down anything that you want to remember – any images, messages, connections or feelings. You may not immediately understand the messages you have received, so just let them sink into your consciousness. Meaning may become clearer in the next few days.

BRINGING HEALING INTO THE BODY

Too often we turn away from our bodies when they become sick, feeling disgusted, repulsed, let down, irritated or frustrated. We think we are stupid when we get hurt; that we must be bad when we get ill. The illness becomes something to be overcome or repelled as quickly as possible. However, when we reject the body in this way we often create more pain. For we are rejecting ourselves.

When something is in pain, what does it need most? What is it really crying out for? Is it not to be loved? To be embraced and held? We hold a child in our arms to comfort a grazed knee or soothe a banged elbow, yet when we hurt ourselves we get annoyed, when we get ill we wish the illness would go away. Eddie remembers when he was a child hearing people whispering about a woman who had cancer as if she had done something wrong and was being punished. The only thing we do wrong is to turn against ourselves.

We can decide that we are not going to let the illness destroy us, and this does often bring a cure. For instance, there are many well-documented cases of people who have successfully cured disease through visualizing their healthy cells attacking and overcoming their diseased cells. We can also decide to embrace our pain or disease, to bring it into our being rather than to push it away. In *Healing into Life and Death*, Stephen Levine explains how:

> We noticed that many who seemed unable to heal, instead of embracing their illness, met it with an 'I'm going to beat this thing!' attitude. Most were *at* their illnesses . . . 'me against me', 'me against the pain'. Others, we noticed, were *with* their illness . . . touching it deeply, examining it, drawing the self-torture out of it by meeting it with tenderness and mercy. . . . These were the people who embraced their pain and fear, and met what had always been conditioned by fear and loathing with a new openness, and at times a new wonderment at life.

This is not necessarily effortless. When times are hard it can take all our energy just to breathe. It is easy to become bitter and feel hopeless, to think that nobody understands what we are feeling or going through – the hurt, the fear. It takes courage to face pain, not to become self-defeative. But we can accept what is happening; acknowledging our physical condition and accepting it into our lives, living each moment as it comes. We can relax into the pain, sinking into it as rain sinks into soft earth. We can learn from it, tenderly exploring what it means and what it may be trying to tell us. Breathing and relaxing, we simply listen for the answers, holding ourselves gently, with love.

When it comes to pain, like most people, I am a coward. While lying in bed with intense sinusitis pain in my face and head, my mind kept throwing up all the logical arguments about phoning the doctor and getting something done to stop the pain. But as a nurse I knew this was not a condition I would die from, and I knew enough about natural therapies and relaxation to create a stress-free situation. So I chose to be with the pain on my own. I had to lie very still, as any movement sent arrows of pain shooting deep inside; I covered my head with a towel and entered deeply into the darkness. All around was silence, except for the incessant chatter in my mind!

As I grew stiller, something began to change. My inner voice began to speak to me. 'Be present in the pain.' What did that mean? How could I not be present? Then I realized that the pain was present but that I was constantly finding ways of removing my mind from it, going over all the reasons why I was in this state; slowly I was becoming more and more depressed. 'BE PRESENT.' I began to focus on the pain, breathing into the very centre of the pain. Every time my mind wandered to old thought patterns, the pain intensified. I had to become more and more present. No distractions, just being in the pain. I began to know that the pain was all right. It was OK to have the pain, I was OK within the pain. A process was taking place in my body and I knew I would come out of it intact, whole. Suddenly I knew peace! I was deep, deep within myself in a place of complete and utter peace. There was nothing other than the feeling of total peace in every cell of my body. Here began my real healing.

HELEN HUMPHRIES

Accepting the pain is not a giving up, it does not imply that we do not want to be cured, it is not saying that we have to suffer our fate no matter what happens. But neither is it a pushing away of the illness, or a blaming of it on external factors. When we accept illness as a part of us, as an expression of our whole being, then we see that it is a tremendous opportunity for growth. A chance to change those aspects of our lives that are not working, to let go of past patterns, fears and insecurities. To bring into our lives that which enlivens, uplifts and fulfils, that which is fearless and open-hearted. For illness brings with it its own gifts, its own teachings for us to learn and receive.

The fullness of my healing seemed to be in the gifts that being in pain gave to me. The first gift was the stillness and silence, a chance to be totally present in my being. Then came forgiveness. Forgiveness of myself for the pain, for being fearful, for not facing the problems, for not loving; and forgiveness of others for express- ing their love in unloving ways. From this came a promise to love: to love myself enough to be present in my body, to take time to find answers, to say 'no' when necessary and 'yes' with confidence. The third gift was that of nature – the warmth of the sun, the trees, the moon, the earth – and allowing this into myself. Then came the gift of just being instead of doing, just being with me and being OK with that. And finally came the gift of friendship, as I found the strength to ask for help, and received such unconditional love and support.

HELEN HUMPHRIES

To be fully present is to live and use each day that we have as completely as we can; it is the quality of our lives rather than the quantity. The physical body is impermanent and we will all die at some point, but our healing is not limited in any way. This is what is real and important. Bernie Siegel is a surgeon who believes in the power of love to heal. He talks about the quality of life, of the richness we can bring to our lives and how a loving life gives so much meaning and joy. A television interviewer wanted to know what the statistics were – if the people who focused on hope and love actually lived longer than those who didn't. Bernie replied that he was interested in the quality of their lives, not the quantity.

We say we want to live longer and to be healed, but are we living a quality life? Are we living with love or with bitterness? Do we have to wait until we get signs of a serious illness before we make changes? Before we do what we have always wanted to do? In *Grace and Grit*, Ken Wilber says to his wife Treya:

Since nobody knows what caused your cancer, I don't know what you should change in order to help cure it. So

97

why don't you try this. Why don't you use cancer as a metaphor and a spur to change all those things in your life that you wanted to change anyway. In other words, repressing certain emotions may or may not have helped cause the cancer, but since you want to stop repressing those emotions anyway, then use the cancer as a reason, as an excuse to do so. . . . Why not take the cancer as an opportunity to change all those things that can be changed?

BODYMIND AWARENESS

The following pages can be read as a continuation of this chapter, as each part of the body is described and this will deepen your understanding of the bodymind relationship. Or they can be used as a guided visualization. There are times when you may just want to read it through; at other times you may want to do it as a visualization practice. If you wish, you can also skip directly to the part of the body that you want to focus on in order to spend more time there, communicating, listening, relaxing and loving. Remember, your body hears and believes every word you say!

PRACTICE – Bodymind Awareness Visualization

If there is a part of your body that is not well, then as you come to that part in the visualization, spend more time there. You may want to develop a dialogue with this part, to ask if there are any messages for you, if there is anything it would like to tell you. In order for your body to heal, it may need you to do something specific to help release the pain. See if you can establish a communication with your wounded parts, so that your understanding of yourself can deepen.

This practice should be done lying down, using a small pillow for your head and a blanket to keep you warm. You

---

can even play some very soft, gentle, relaxing music. Arms should be parallel to the body, palms upward. Feet are slightly apart. Eyes are closed.

Feel yourself completely relaxing, your body becoming heavier as it sinks into the floor. Focus on the flow of the breath as it enters and leaves, watching the flow, breathing naturally with the flow. Do this for a few minutes – simply moving with the flow of your breath, feeling your body rise and fall with each breath.

Feet
Now bring your attention to your feet. With your mind, feel each of your toes . . . the soles of your feet . . . the arch . . . the top of your feet. . . . Seek out any tension and let it go. Become aware of what your feet do for you; how they carry you through your life; how they keep you grounded, walking on the earth; how they are the part of you that goes first into the world, giving direction and purpose. If the terrain of your life becomes very rough, then it is your feet that take the first knocks. Thank your feet for all they do, feel gratitude for the love they unconditionally offer you through their service, breathe into your feet.

Ankles
Now bring your attention to your ankles. Such tiny parts, yet they keep you upright and stable. They are a bridge between your mind, your body and the earth, that which enables the mind to find its place in the world. When an ankle collapses, your whole being gives way, as if your support system has collapsed or let you down. Sometimes the feet want to go in one direction but your mind is going in a different direction, and your ankles get caught in the middle. Conflict can be expressed in your ankles when the direction you are going in is changing; when the ground beneath you feels like quicksand; when your support system is collapsing; or when you are finding it hard to stand up for yourself. Thank your ankles for all that they

do, for the support they give you, the strength they need in order to do this, and the love they share as they hold you upright in the world.

Calves and Shin Bones

Now bring your attention to your calves and shin bones. Breathe into any tension and let it go. How many times have you bruised or banged your shin bones when you are about to be going in a direction that you are not sure you want to go in? Or is the ground beneath you beginning to look very rough and movement becoming difficult? Do you fear you will be let down in some way? The lower part of your legs holds all this energy. Embrace your shin bones and calf muscles in your heart; thank them for all they do.

Knees

Now bring your attention to your knees. Dear, beloved knees that go through so much in their lifetime! They are your ability to bend, to be flexible. Kneeling is an act of surrendering the ego, of recognizing higher authority. Difficulty with the knees may mean you are having a hard time accepting or surrendering to a situation. The knees are also your shock absorbers, taking all the pressure of your being in relation to the terrain you are walking on, the changes being experienced. The knees allow you to move with flexibility, and they easily get stiff if you become inflexible in your mind. Deeply thank your knees for all that they do, for the love they give in their service, for the years of hard work they offer. Breathe into your knees.

Thighs

Now bring your attention to your thighs. Such quiet strength here. Seek out any tension and breathe into it. As you grow into adulthood, you move away from your parents and family and your thighs represent this movement. They are connected to your relationship to your mother or father, and to any repressed or hidden feelings.

Your thighs are also closely connected to the expression of your sexuality, to the degree of freedom you feel to be open and responsive with another person. Thank your thighs for the love they give you, as they enable you to walk on your own in this world and to share yourself with others. Breathe deeply into your thighs.

Legs and Feet in Their Entirety
Feel both your legs and feet in their entirety and thank them for the work they do. How they enable you to stand upright. To hold your own ground and place in the world. To walk forwards, to run and jump, to move, to dance. To feel the earth always beneath you, giving direction and purpose. Thank you, legs, I love you! Feel the warmth of your love pouring through your legs as you breathe into them.

Genitals
Now bring your attention to your genitals. Gently, tenderly, let your heart open to your genitals. Accept all the feelings that may arise as you enter into this area. Keep breathing and relaxing. Become aware of the whole of your reproductive organs. Your genitals and reproductive organs are intimately connected to your deepest feelings about your sexuality; about how you may have been abused; feelings about having or not having children; difficulties in sharing your sexuality, communicating and being intimate; or issues of insecurity, failure, guilt and self-dislike. Breathe deeply. Take your time. Acknowledge whatever arises, and let it go. With great tenderness, thank your genitals for their love for you, for the joy they give you, soften any tension there and let your love flow.

Buttocks and Anus
Now bring your attention to your buttocks and your anus. This is where you sit on all those things you want no one else to see! Release the tension here and breathe into it.

This area is to do with elimination and expresses your inner tension and stress. The anus muscles hold tight whenever you feel nervous, when you resist change or spontaneity, instead becoming fixed or even stubborn. When you feel out of control of your reality or feel pushed into new situations, this is where the tension will be found. Breathe into the tension and let it go. Thank your buttocks and your anus for serving you, feel the love and rejoice in that love.

Pelvis

Now bring your attention to your pelvis, the ring of bone that holds and supports your whole being. The pelvis is the centre of movement of your body. It gives direction to the legs and support to the spine. The pelvis allows you to stand upright and strong on your legs. Within the pelvis is where you share your sexuality, give birth, digest your food, release waste. These are very basic instinctive expressions, connected with your sense of survival and security. Difficulties here can indicate a confusion in direction; a fear of being left or standing alone; a pulling back and a resistance to sharing yourself; or a sense of insecurity. Thank your pelvis, which so silently holds your whole being in a ring of strength and love. Thank it deeply, breathing into it.

Spine

Now bring your attention to your spine, stretching from the pelvis upwards to your neck. Feel the whole of your back as it lies on the floor – the muscles, the ribs, the different vertebrae. Breathe into your back, into each bone, each sinew. The back is where you tend to put everything that you do not want to look at, the place where your buried feelings and painful experiences can be found. Here are issues to do with power and control, without which you may feel 'spineless'; with maturing and growing older gracefully, or with resistance and clinging;

102

with fulfilling your purpose and direction, or getting trapped in meaningless ruts; with justice and standing up for yourself, or with accepting injustice. Any tension in this area will affect the whole of your body.

The spine is the backbone of your life: it gives you dignity and pride, your ability to walk freely and with uprightness. It is the pillar upon which the rest of your being is built. Feel your back and deeply thank each part of it for the years of service it has unconditionally given you, for the love with which it supports you each day. Breathe into your spine. Relax your shoulder blades. Let your love pour through every part of your back.

Kidneys and Bladder
Now bring your attention to your lower abdomen and the organs contained there. Start with your kidneys and bladder. This wonderful waste disposal system goes on all the time, cleansing and keeping you refreshed. It is the area that enables you to let go of all the negative feelings you no longer need. If difficulties arise here, then see if there are any unhappy, resentful, fearful or angry feelings that you need to release. Feel the work that this area does so unconditionally, lovingly, so that you may stay balanced. Thank your kidneys and bladder deeply for their love.

Pancreas and Spleen
Now bring your attention to the pancreas and the spleen and feel how these organs are always maintaining the sugar balance in your body so that you may stay sweet; with the love in your being always available, always flowing. The spleen is also connected to your immune system and sense of self-protection. Thank these organs for the love they give to you. Breathe in and out of these organs and feel their love for you.

Liver
Now bring your attention to your liver, that which

maintains and preserves life. The blessed liver, always purifying, cleansing, detoxifying, keeping you strong. Breathe into your liver. Feel any toxins being released. Your liver suffers if you become addicted to alcohol or fatty food, when you get excessively angry or repress your anger. Deeply thank your liver for being so concerned about your health that it works tirelessly for you to stay balanced, loving you so unconditionally.

Colon and Intestines

Now bring your attention to your colon and intestines. This extraordinary part of your being that not only absorbs and utilizes nourishment from the food you eat and releases that which you no longer need, but also absorbs your reality, integrating and processing all the things that are happening to you, letting go of that which is finished with. If the reality you are swallowing is hard to digest, all sorts of intestinal difficulties can arise. If it does not contain the nourishment you need, you may feel depleted, lack energy and be unable to give, no matter how well you eat. Breathe into and release any tension in your intestines. Keep your belly soft. Thank your intestines for the work they so tirelessly do, absorbing, digesting, keeping you nourished and sustained. Thank them and feel their unconditional love for you, let your love pour through them.

Stomach

Now bring your attention to your stomach. This is where your digestive processes begin, where your outer reality and your inner reality meet, where all your longings, desires, pressures and conflicts are assimilated. How you feel about your life is connected to how you feel in your stomach: if it feels empty and needs filling, if it feels lonely and needs comforting, if it feels stressed and needs calming, or if it feels overfilled and needs to be cleansed.

104

Breathe into your stomach. Feel a softness and gentleness there. Thank your stomach for the love it gives you so constantly, so unconditionally.

Lungs
Now bring your attention to your lungs. The gift of life is given to you in the very breath you take, and your lungs then send that breath throughout your body. Your lungs are connected to your desire to live – this is where you say 'yes' to life, or where you retract and retreat. When your lungs are not well, see if you have something you need to get off your chest, some deep feelings that are not getting fully expressed, or perhaps something you are taking in is causing you irritation. Breathe into your lungs and notice if you breathe in a shallow way, staying near the surface, uncommitted; then breathe deeply, filling your whole lungs and letting it out slowly. See how this releases tension throughout your entire being. Through your breath you nourish every cell, bringing awareness and life. Feel the love in your lungs as they breathe. Thank your lungs for their love.

Heart and Blood
Now bring your attention to your heart. This blessed, loving, tender centre of your being. Breathe into your heart. With each breath feel your heart opening, softening, releasing. Surrounding your heart there may be many layers of pain, rejection, hurt or abuse, but as you soften these and find your way through, within your heart lies the greatest of riches, a wealth of love that embraces all the pain. This is the centre of love, of fearlessness, of compassion, the passageway to the very core of your being. Take the fearlessness in your heart and embrace your fear; use the love to embrace your hurt and pain. Breathe into your heart that it may open, that the compassion may spill forth to touch all those it meets. Unconditionally, constantly, your heart pumps life-sustaining

105

blood throughout your body.

As your heart is the centre of love within you, so your blood is that love as it circulates throughout your whole being, throughout your world. The blood carries your love, feeding and nourishing each cell with that love. It is connected to your ability to give love as well as receive it, to feeling life in your whole being or to wanting to withdraw or contract emotionally. Thank your heart and the blood. Thank them for the life they give you, for the love that is stored there, for the unconditional love always serving you.

Breasts

Now bring your attention to your breasts. For a woman there is tenderness and sensitivity, nourishment, sustenance and comfort here. Feelings about being a woman, having children, about sexuality and attractiveness. For a man there is strength, power and bravery in the chest, as well as protection and gentleness. Feelings about being masculine enough, being strong or weak. This area, in both men and women, is connected to your most intimate feelings about yourself. No part of the human body is so agonized over, so worshipped, nor so exposed. Breathe into any resistances and let them go. Find that place in yourself that can embrace your breasts, that can accept and love yourself just as you are. Thank your breasts, your chest, for the love that is there, that nourishes and protects you. Such unconditional, nurturing love. Breathe into your chest and release any tension there.

Hands

Now bring your attention to your hands. Let your mind feel its way through each of your fingers, the palms, and the back of your hands. Through the hands you share and extend yourself, you create. Here you show how you are handling life or are being handled. You do so much with your hands, but is it what you want to be doing? With the

106

hands you communicate acceptance or rejection of another, you show tenderness or resistance. They are your antennae, reaching out into the world and testing the response that is given. They are the furthest reaching expression of yourself. Are they reaching where you want to go? Hold your hands with gratitude. Thank them for being there, for the service they give so consistently, so lovingly, breathe into your hands.

Wrists

Now bring your attention to your wrists which allow for so much movement of expression. They are the bridge between your heart and your hands. Through them you can bring alive your words as you talk, you can dance, you can hold and caress. Your wrists are connected to your flexibility or rigidity in all expression, and to whether you feel at ease or stressful about what you are doing. Do they pull or tighten, are they relaxed and loose? Breathe into your wrists. Thank your wrists for letting the energy flow freely through them, for serving you with love, for expressing your love.

Forearms

Now bring your attention to your forearms. Breathe into your forearms. Your energy comes through this area before being expressed in your hands, so the forearms hold any uncertainties or doubts you may have just as you are about to do something. Let them relax and be at ease. The forearms enable you to express yourself more fully. Breathe in and out with awareness. Thank your forearms for their work, so silently and constantly, loving you deeply.

Elbows

Now bring your attention to your elbows. Through your elbows you can bend and move your arms, you can lift, embrace, pull; you can also push away or push through

107

with the elbows. They allow for grace in your movement, for flexibility in your activity, for freedom in your expression. Thank your elbows for giving you so much, for unconditionally loving you. Breathe deeply into your elbows.

Upper Arms
Now bring your attention to your upper arms. Here lies much of your strength and endurance, the power to express yourself fully in the world. Through the arms you can hold and care for another, you can reach out to embrace; or you can pull back and close them to form a protective barrier – the upper arms give strength here. They can also support others and provide a safe haven to rest under. Thank your upper arms for their durability and strength, for holding and loving you so gently. Feel your love embrace them, as they embrace you, and let your breath flow through them.

Shoulders
Now bring your attention to your shoulders. Here, where you carry the world and its problems, where your own difficulties lie heavy, and where your longing to express yourself may be held back by fear. Breathe deeply into your shoulders and release any tension. Are you really doing what you most want to do? Are you freely expressing yourself, or are you allowing stress and tension to dominate? Are you entering into life or pulling back from it? Are you taking on other people's problems and not even looking at your own? Here you express your attitude to life, whether relaxed or tense; and here your feelings for others are shown, whether warm and inviting or cold and withdrawn. Breathe and relax. Thank your shoulders for the load they carry, for the work they do, through which they show their love for you. Love your shoulders, feel a warmth pouring through them and down your arms.

Neck

Now bring your attention to your neck, the bridge between your head and heart. Through the neck you take in nourishment – food, water, air – that keeps your body alive; your thoughts and ideas are transmitted through the neck to find expression in the body; and you express your heartfelt feelings through your voice. Here also you swallow your reality, taking in the feelings and sensations from the world around you; and here you may swallow back your feelings when they appear inappropriate or wrong or are rejected. This can result in a very painful throat and neck if the unexpressed energy builds up.

Your neck, this tender and vulnerable part of your being that can be hurt so easily, is also connected to your openness and ability to see on all sides, to being receptive and responsive; or to being closed, stiff and rigid, stubbornly seeing only what lies right in front of you. There can also be a split between the mind and the body when, locked in your mind, you become separated from the feelings in the body, out of touch with your heart and the love that is there. Breathe into your neck. Feel it relax and let go. It does not need to hold tightly. Feel the love your neck has for you, holding your head high, taking in nourishment, connecting your mind and body. Thank your neck for its strength and love, for its flexibility and openness.

Head

Now bring your attention to your head. Your centre of communication and intelligence, from which you experience the world through your senses, understand the world through your brain, and experience the higher realms through your inner perception. Each part of your head plays its role to perfection, creating a harmony of brilliance. Thank your head for being such a warm and loving host to your spirit, for its intelligence and receptivity. Thank it for caring for you and watching out for you, for making decisions and understanding so well, for maintaining your body and physical health. Breathe into your head, this wonderful centre of communication.

Eyes

Now bring your attention to the individual parts of the head. Firstly your eyes, through which you see, and through which you are seen. If what you are seeing around or ahead of you is not what you want to see, then you may withdraw your sight or have problems seeing clearly. Or you may not want others to see into you through your eyes, for the eyes express all your feelings, whether positive or negative. Tears are the waters of healing. Thank your tears for the healing they bring, for all the feelings they express. When you see clearly, the world is not only beautiful but your perception is sharper and the inner eye awakens. Thank your eyes for their brightness, their vision, that gives you so much joy. Breathe into your eyes. Feel the love your eyes have for you.

Ears

Now bring your attention to your ears, that special place of hearing, of perceiving your world through sound. Too often what you hear may cause discomfort and a pain inside, an ache or infection. In the ears you also find your equilibrium, enabling your life to be in harmony. Is there an imbalance in your life? Thank your ears for the sound of life they bring to you, the glorious sounds and the painful sounds, all making a whole. Thank them for the love they show in keeping you poised and graceful in your movement. Breathe into your ears and feel the love.

Nose

Now bring your awareness to your nose. Here the scent of life, the many smells that bring the world alive around you, enter your being. Here also you breathe and bring precious oxygen into your lungs. But here also you get colds and a runny nose! If this happens, see if there is some crying, grieving or tears that need to be shed. Crying and having a runny nose share many of the same symptoms. And if you have a blocked nose, see if there is perhaps an aspect of your life you are wanting to block out, not to breathe in. Thank your nose for the sweet smells that fill your being, for the oxygen that fills your lungs. Feel the love your nose has for you in its tireless activity of breathing and smelling. Breathe in new breath to your nose.

Mouth

Now bring your attention to your mouth. So many activities take place here. In your mouth you taste food as it enters and you taste reality as it first appears. You may not like the taste and refuse to swallow, or it may make your mouth feel bitter, hot or even blistered. Here also you speak, sharing the depths of your being with others, singing, talking, whispering, or perhaps holding back what you might want to say. Are you saying what you want to say? With the mouth you share your love with your kisses and endearments, also receiving here the love from another. Are you kissing the right person? In the mouth, your teeth begin to break down your food and see what is there, rejecting what is not wanted. They act as a gateway through which reality has to pass. When the reality is not welcome, you clench your teeth and set your jaw. Nothing may enter! Nothing can exit either, so unexpressed anger or fear may be found in your jaw. Thank your mouth, teeth and jaw for their love, for the constant service they give you. Breathe into them, releasing any tension.

The Whole Body

Now hold your whole body in your love. Feel the bones, the muscles, the flesh, the skin. Feel how they are serving

111

you with love. Feel your hair and nails. Feel your nerves that communicate throughout your being, the glands and the immune system protecting you. Feel your tears, saliva, urine, blood, sweat and all the other precious liquids within you. Feel their deep love for you, and feel your love for them pouring through you.

Now bring your attention to the energy within you, flowing throughout your being: your life force. Feel the power of this life force. Breathe deeply into your life force and become one with it as it pulsates throughout you. Feel the love and the healing in your breath. Discover the healing power you have within yourself through your breath. With each inward breath feel life filling your being. Visualize yourself as whole, as healed. Silently repeat to yourself, 'May I be well. May all of me be well. May the healing power of love be with me always.'

6

LOVING
RELATIONSHIPS

*The love you take
is equal to the love you make.*
THE BEATLES

Relationships, whether with ourselves, another person or even the planet as a whole, form the foundation of our existence. For as long as there is life there is relationship. There can never be just one, alone, always there is one in relationship to and with another. The cells of our body exist through relationship with every other cell, just as we exist in relationship with other humans, with animals, plants, rain, the sun, moon and stars, and with the air we breathe.

Ultimately the relationship we have with ourselves is the basis for all other relationships; how we feel about ourselves influences and determines how we react or respond to others and the world around us. The state of our relationships therefore reflects, like a mirror, where we are at in ourselves. If we are not at ease or do not like ourselves, then no matter what happens we will find something to complain about or will focus on what is wrong. If we have made friends and are at ease with ourselves, then we will enjoy life and feel a gratitude for what we have; when times are hard we will have a greater ability to be cheerful and to remain peaceful.

When we pull back into a sense of separateness, then we blame external things for our problems, we think in terms of 'them and us'. There is no acknowledgement that relationship is a two-way affair, that we are equally involved. When we remember our basic interdependence and our shared humanity, then we reconnect with our essential unity.

Yet, at the same time as being so inter-related and interdependent, each member of the human race is also unique and complete and very different from the next in the way he or she thinks, acts, feels, in his or her motivations, goals and ideologies. Rarely do more than a few of us think the same way about the same thing at the same time: we have different moods and temperaments, different likes and dislikes. The fact that we can get on with each other sometimes seems miraculous!

I was a monk in India, a swami, and felt that my life was dedicated to finding the truth. This meant to me, at the time, that if I was on the path to liberation then an intimate relationship with another person would only be a distraction. For me the path was a solitary one. The world was an illusion filled with pain and suffering. It seemed that desire always brought pain and so I wanted out. Yet when I met Debbie, some years later, it was clear that the next phase of my life was to be with her. I was outwardly at ease but inwardly I felt somewhat unsure. I had been so long with myself and now I had to contend with someone else. When I was alone I never had to answer to anyone, I knew what was important to me and had no need to compromise. In relationship all manner of things arise to cause conflict – two minds do not always think alike! Even more so as I am American and Debbie is English. At times it felt it would have been easier if we spoke different languages, times when we thought we were understanding each other only to find out we were talking about different things!

After we were married we went to India to be with our teachers. We were sitting with the Dalai Lama in his palace in Dharmsala, and I was so moved by this gentle, simple, loving man that I just wanted to stay close. I didn't want to leave the extraordinary

114

wisdom emanating from such a delightful being. So I said, 'I don't want to leave, I want to stay here with you.' And the Dalai Lama replied, 'If we were together all the time, we would quarrel!' What a great teaching.

EDDIE

Our relationships with each other dominate and influence every aspect of our lives. Through them we find ourselves, know ourselves and can explore our highest potential. We learn from our relationships – they provide the opportunity to gain valuable insights into ourselves and each other. They give us the greatest joy yet cause us the greatest concern. Even when we are alone we are in relationship with ourselves and the world around us; we have the opportunity to get to know ourselves in a special way, to become our own best friend.

If we are maintaining relationships that are unloving or unsupportive, even abusive, fearful or disrespectful, then such relationships will keep us in a state of separation and confusion. Where there is fear there cannot be love; where there is no love, the heart cannot be open. Healing is needed. Honest, caring, kind and respectful relationships, with both ourselves and with others, give us the ground from which we can grow, they create the space for the heart to blossom.

INTO ME YOU SEE

A healthy relationship with another person involves our ability to let go of our defences and become intimate. It is entering into a bond of trust. Allowing another to know us, to touch our feelings, to experience us where we are most vulnerable, to share our strengths and weaknesses. Intimacy can sound so romantic and sensual, it is so desired, yet it often triggers incredible fear, irrational behaviour and a complete shutdown of feelings. Rather than entering into the longed-for experience of ultimate closeness, we can find ourselves retreating back into our separate selves.

Real intimacy is not necessarily the same as sexual intimacy. Indeed, sexual closeness is often mistaken for intimacy, but it rarely guarantees that real intimacy will develop. To understand this further it helps to see how intimacy can mean 'into me you see', for when we get close to another we are seen for who we really are. If we are not at ease or on friendly terms with ourselves, then inevitably we feel exposed and naked, fear takes over and we want to run away. Times in the past when we were hurt, abused or rejected all add to our resistance and we withdraw. An invisible wall comes up, one that has been carefully constructed in order to stop further rejection or hurt. However, this wall also stops us from being able to feel or express our deeper feelings – it keeps us isolated within ourselves. Then intimacy becomes even harder to achieve.

To reach that place where we can sink into intimacy, where we can breathe into the fear so that we enter defenceless and open into relationship, means being intimate with ourselves – 'into me I see'. As we acknowledge and accept the many facets of our being and we come to know ourselves more deeply, then we have less to hide. This does not mean that we have to overcome all our issues and become completely free of conflict before we can enter into relationship; we do not have to wait until we are perfect! All the hidden monsters don't just pack up and leave overnight. It is simply that we start to accept ourselves as we are, to get on more friendly terms with what is there.

To achieve an honest and genuine relationship with another person we therefore need to start by developing an intimate relationship with ourselves, a friendship and ease with who we are. When this friendship is established it allows our friendships with others to be more spacious and durable. For we know ourselves, we know our monsters and their particular peculiarities, we know our limitations and where we have yet to grow.

Developing a friendship with ourselves means finding out how we think and feel and what our own beliefs are. It means listening to our own wisdom. It is about respecting and honouring who we are, just as we are. A loving friendship with ourselves is the most important relationship we can have.

116

It feels like disaster has struck. I am desolate. Lydia told me, at the airport when I went to meet her, that she wants to end the relationship, she needs to cut out and have her space. I feel awful. Reminded of all the times I was left, or rejected, all the times my fondest hopes were dashed. Yet at the same time I understand; I feel myself much stronger and clearer about who I am, who my little boy is and how to look after him and heal him. I want to continue the relationship with Lydia because I love her very much – she is a fantastic woman – but right now I have to see it as over so I don't torture myself with false hope. I feel kind of empty, yet I also know that this is a part of the most important process of my life, in that FINALLY I'm getting close to learning that love is within me, not outside of me. I have the choice, which is more conscious than it ever was, to choose to love myself and accept my own love, to bathe in the golden fountain within me, or to turn away again in fear and sorrow and believe once more that it is out of reach. I am trying to remember right now that nothing is lost, save perhaps some illusions I held, and that sad and happy are a choice.

DAVE HAMPTON

TIME OUT: To Make Friends with Yourself

Whether or not you are in a primary relationship, if you feel out of touch with your inner being take some time out now to make friends with yourself. Have some paper and a pen with you. Take a few minutes to settle and become quiet. Watch the flow of your breath as it comes and goes. Have your eyes closed. When you are ready, ask the following questions. Let the answers arise freely. Write them down if you want to. You may prefer to do this in a notebook, starting each page with a different question.

- Do I feel comfortable with myself?
- Can I spend time alone and enjoy myself?
- If not, why not?
- What would I most like to do with time alone?

117

- What does it mean to be a friend to myself?
- Am I friendly to others, or do I expect them to be friendly first?
- Do I shy away from being intimate?
- Do I respect my own feelings, or am I easily swayed by other people?
- Do I express my own ideas, or do I feel they are not worth it?
- Do I care about myself?
- When I am alone, do I eat well or do I binge?
- Do I love myself?

Ask yourself any other questions you may want to. Being a friend to yourself involves taking time to honour and respect your own being. You cannot be a friend to yourself or to anyone else if you do not care about yourself. When we express how we feel it releases the pressure inside. Take time to talk to yourself and get to know who you are.

LOVE BRINGS UP EVERYTHING THAT ISN'T LOVE!

An intimate relationship is a great healer, for it provides a safe space for pain to be soothed and torment to be eased. Love brings up everything that isn't love, in order that it be healed. All the hidden pain from past abuse, repressed feelings, inadequacies, insecurities, fear, shame, denial – they all arise so they may be released and healed. This is our opportunity to become whole.

However, the arrival of such long-repressed aspects of ourselves can obviously create a strain on both partners. Not all relationships survive this. Great amounts of selfless patience and tolerance are needed, especially when we may not understand what is happening. Now, more than ever, do we need to remember to breathe, to keep going forward with fearlessness, embracing even that which appears unembraceable. True intimacy accepts all aspects of the other person; there cannot be a pushing away or denial of any part, for that will preclude wholeness.

> *Eddie and I met at a time when I had been on my own for a while, healing from a past relationship and discovering who I was for myself. I remember looking out of the window at a beautiful icicle and realizing that I felt whole, that I had made friends with who I was and I deeply valued this friendship. It was a sense of relief at having come home to myself. Eddie and I met a week later and were together from then on.*
>
> *We believed we both knew ourselves, that we had nothing to hide from ourselves or each other, so there should be no difficulties. But the intimacy took us a step further and exposed all those corners where we hadn't looked; it brought up issues we thought were already healed but where we still needed to go deeper. Pain that had happened years previously was suddenly alive again, stopping me in my tracks, creating an emotional roller coaster. I realized that, although I had made friends with my present, I now needed to make friends with my past. At the same time, Eddie was dealing with his own issues to do with trust and commitment. It took us a while to find solid ground together!*
>
> DEBBIE

Communication is the core of all relationships; how we communicate with each other, how we feel about another's communication to us, how much we are able to share, how much we hold back, how well we are able to express our feelings, how much in touch we are with what we are feeling, what we think someone else is feeling, what we think has been said, what was actually said, what was not said, what was implied. Without communication the difficulties grow: the hidden resentments, secret feelings, fantasies of what another might or might not feel, the 'I'm right but he/she is wrong' syndrome.

If there is any form of deceit, power struggle, manipulation or resistance in the relationship then it will act like quicksand, pulling us down. To bring healing into the picture, we must take time to air the issues and talk. To really see what is causing such conflict and how we can bring about a resolution. Perhaps we have allowed someone to have control over us and now we feel powerless; maybe something happened in a relationship that has never been talked about, creating a barrier in our ability to communicate; or perhaps someone has been making constant demands on us and we have not yet found the words to stop them.

For so often the ego gets in the way and hinders the process of communication. It is as if, when we first become intimate, the egos dissolve into each other and we become one. Then we are in harmony and this works wonderfully! But if fear, anger or selfishness is present, then such intimacy will make the ego rear up its head. This causes us to pull back and retreat into our separate corners, the ego intact again and communication at a standstill. In moments of conflict it is as if the ego becomes hardened – like a rock, it will *not* give way! As we are still so close there is now the tendency to start bumping into each other, one ego knocking heads with the other ego, all the while trying to find again that place of merging and harmony.

If a relationship is not working we tend either to blame the other person involved or to blame ourselves. One of us must be wrong! However, this will not bring about healing or reconciliation. Instead, it is necessary for both partners to acknowledge how each is contributing to the situation, perhaps through unconsciously stimulating the conflict, by playing the victim role, by reacting from past experiences, by denying real feelings, or by not communicating with honesty and openness. Perhaps, even, by withdrawing altogether, maintaining a passivity and refusal to share or talk at all. June told us how whenever she and her partner, Barry, came near a disagreement he would simply retreat. She could not engage him in any way. When this happens there is no space to move. There has to be a willingness to work together and a care for each other. Without that basic care, any reconciliation will not last.

A very hard lesson I once learned was that conflict cannot be resolved in an atmosphere where the parties involved have lost basic appreciation for each other. In such an atmosphere you can get a settlement, an 'acceptable solution', but you do not get real reconciliation which involves a re-establishment of appreciation for each other as human beings. I was sharing a house with two other men. We were friendly enough. Then one day conflict began about the typical house issues which people who share houses get into. One issue sparked another until anger and hurt escalated and we became totally alienated from each other, a 'cold war' had begun. Eventually we had to have a meeting because there were real practical issues to be dealt with. The meeting was horrible — steely voices, eyes shooting poisoned darts. An acceptable solution was eventually reached.

But a few days later, in the shower, I vomited for over an hour until my throat was so raw my voice was totally lost. What was my responsibility? What was my part in giving birth to this monster? As I searched my soul deeply for the answer, it became clear that the moment at which I had created the conditions for irreconcilability far predated the actual onset of any conflict. The turning point was when I had ceased to appreciate the other two men. I had started being judgmental, devaluing them. This failure to regard them with positive value was the real start of the trouble. When people have esteem for each other, then, when there is conflict they are motivated to solve things, to re-establish the relationship. Without that esteem or appreciation, there is no motivation for lasting resolution.

ARON GERSH

Just as a good workman never blames his tools when his work does not go right, so blaming either part of the relationship does little to solve the situation. It simply causes further conflict. Recognizing the underlying behaviour, attitudes and feelings, unconscious motivations and influences, will do more to bring healing than will recrimination and blame. For very often we are simply repeating patterns we learned from our parents or from past experiences; getting angry or pulling back may have nothing to do with our partner, but is a reflection of unresolved limitations in need of healing.

This process is encouraged by an attitude of looking within ourselves, rather than looking at someone else and expecting them to change. Once we accept that, basically, we cannot change anyone else, cannot *make* them be different, and that the only thing we can change is our attitude towards them, then healing becomes possible. This is the hardest reality to accept, as we can see another's faults far more easily than our own. It seems obvious where someone else may need to change or how they could do things better. Surely working with our own attitude is not the point, for we are not wrong! It is so much easier to point the finger at someone else and demand they do the changing. But when you point a finger, take a moment to notice that there are actually three fingers pointing back at you! The following story shares the advice offered to us for working with difficulties in relationship:

> *Shortly after our marriage we were given some invaluable advice by Akong Rinpoche, the abbot of Samye Ling, a Tibetan Buddhist monastery in Scotland. Debbie and I had only met six months previously and we were still getting to know each other. Akong suggested that if we start to disagree or argue, then we should take some time out for ourselves to consider what we are doing. Rather than complaining about how the other person is treating us, we should look at our own behaviour and the effect it is having, we should explore our own motives, attitudes and hidden agendas. How am I treating this person? How can I treat them better? What am I doing to him/her? When we come back together again, we can discuss our discoveries if we want, but it isn't necessary as long as we put them into practice.*
>
> EDDIE

Being able to communicate honestly and openly means being fearless and courageous, and if such communication was easy then the world would probably not be in the state it is today. Heads of countries would be talking instead of fighting, the elderly would not be left to die alone, families would not be cut off from each other, there would be less prejudice. When we asked the Dalai Lama what was most needed in the world, he replied, 'People from different races, different countries and different cultures need to come together and talk, to communicate. Then they will see that we are really no different, that we are all each other's brother and sister.'

The rise of the women's liberation movement in the sixties, and the more recent development of the men's movement, are signs of the need to learn about new ways to communicate. For instance, more men are beginning to talk with other men in an open-hearted way, making it important to have time together. They discuss issues such as touching, holding and hugging each other without embarrassment or feeling that it is odd. They talk about how to care and show feelings, how to heal relationships with their fathers, brothers and sons. Eddie was once interviewed in the *Guardian* newspaper. There was a quarter-page photo of him hugging another man with the caption: 'Hug Warriors Aim to Conquer Male Guilt with a Caress'!

The old ways have failed to satisfy us, failed to meet our real needs. In the past, couples would stay together no matter whether they disliked each other or barely spoke – they played out their roles for better or worse. But now we want to understand more deeply, to find ways to let the barriers down and bring healing; we want to explore who we really are as individuals. Traditional roles have become inter-related, re-sponsibilities are mixed and neither role can be easily defined. All these new forms of communication are causing the break-down of old views, customs and values. This gives us a chance to explore non-traditional ways, to deepen our understanding of the complexity of relationship, to get clearer on our values and to become more honest and direct.

TIME OUT: To Look at Relationships

Take some time to look at each of your primary relation-ships, whether with your partner, family members or friends. Honesty is vital! Over the years we easily slip into patterns of behaviour that mask what is actually taking place. Relationships become habitual and repetitive; they can lose their magic and tenderness. For healing to occur we need to be honest and clear with ourselves.

Have some paper and a pen with you. Take a few minutes to become quiet, focusing on your breathing, just watching the natural flow of your breath. Then, one at a

---

time, bring each of your major relationships into your heart. Begin to look at the relationship, at its strengths and weaknesses. Write down whatever you feel you want to. (The following questions can be asked about your partner, your family members or your friends. Simply add the name of the person as appropriate.)

- Am I good friends with X?
- How can I be a better friend?
- Do I feel supported and nourished by our relationship?
- Do I wish X would behave differently?
- Have I told X how I feel about his/her behaviour?
- Am I being selfish?
- Do X and I support each other's interests, even if they are different?
- Do I embarrass X or am I embarrassed by him/her?
- Do I feel I give and receive equally in our relationship?
- Can X and I talk honestly and openly with each other?
- Do we take time to be together?
- Can I tell X my deepest feelings?
- What would I most like to change in our relationship?
- What is needed for this change to happen?
- Am I treating X fairly? Lovingly?
- Have I said, 'I love you' recently?

Ask whatever other questions you need to, in order to get a clear picture of what is happening. Be objective. There is no judgement here, just observation. Take the time to look at each of the relationships that are important to you. Look at the communication you have, the honesty, the openness, the love you share. Try to see where your relationship is working and where it is not. Then see how you might be able to improve it.

LISTENING BETWEEN THE WORDS

Communicating means talking and listening; we cannot really communicate unless we are truly being heard. To listen is to be really present for each other, without diagnosis, analysis, help, guidance or advice. Just a beingness of togetherness, an inviting and accepting presence, an active presence. The need to be heard, to be listened to, is enormous. We need them to hear not the facts but the real story, the one inside the public story, the one we live with inside ourselves.

When our story is really heard by someone else it creates a healing; it releases the charge. When we are heard, we no longer have anything to be ashamed of. Someone else knows: we are not alone. We can breathe more easily. In *Fire in the Heart*, Roger Housden says: 'Speech, the very faculty which can deaden a relationship and preclude any hope of intimacy whatsoever, is at the same time that which can give power and form to the inarticulate whisperings of the heart.'

To be able to listen to another also means being able to hear ourselves. For often our own pain stops us from really hearing another's story of suffering. There is little room in us for their pain as well as our own. But if we do not take time to listen to each other then we easily become isolated and separate. Communication breaks down. Perhaps that is why psychotherapists are in such demand – their job is simply to listen, really to hear what is happening. For that is what we need – a listening ear, not an advice-giving or judging ear! As the trust builds, we can speak more freely. Listening is a vital part of relationship. Too often when there is a breakdown in communication the listening stops. We are no longer hearing each other, only ourselves and our own story. There are two exercises at the end of this chapter to help develop such communication and listening skills.

To listen means to be present, not distracted by other things or by our thoughts, but to be fully here and now. It can be very helpful to set a certain amount of time aside with our partner/children/colleagues/relatives/friends, just to listen to each other. Perhaps an hour a week. Each of us needs to find what works best. During this time we take it in turns, maybe ten minutes each, to talk while the other person listens. Then we reverse roles and the one who listened gets to talk and be heard. This is particularly useful if there are difficulties in the relationship that need to be resolved.

However, it is essential that the one who is listening does not interrupt, respond (even nodding is a judgement), get defensive, try to make themselves right or to fix the situation. He/she is there just to listen, without fidgeting, tapping fingers or moving toes. After both have had their say, then feedback and discussion can take place. Roger Housden continues,

> We find it necessary – invaluable even – to take half an hour most days to make our speaking more conscious. We sit facing each other and are attentive while we each in turn speak on our relationship, on our feelings for each other and for life, and on anything we may have been holding back from each other. In this way we encourage each other to use speech as a vehicle for truth.

When we really listen to someone else, what we hear is not the words or the story – we are hearing between the words and listening with our heart to the inner story. It is very powerful. There is so much more to be heard. In between the different emotions lies a deeper feeling – one of sadness and joy, a longing for freedom, and for merging of self with other.

WRITING DOWN THE WORDS

Apart from talking and listening, there is a third way we can use words to bring healing to ourselves and our relationships. Writing is immensely therapeutic, a means of recognizing and releasing, but in such a way that it is there to be referred to, remembered, clarified and developed. It is a relief. You may have already experienced this while doing some of the Time Out exercises in earlier chapters, when you wrote down your feelings.

Keeping a journal can be one of the most powerful healing processes. It provides the opportunity to give a voice to our

126

deeper emotions, to clarify elusive feelings and ideas, even to develop a dialogue with those aspects of ourselves that are hidden. When issues become locked in the mind they can seem far greater than they really are or out of proportion to reality. They get repeated over and over until we have no idea what really happened. Writing down our feelings gives us a chance to see clearly: like a fly on the wall, we can observe the dynamics that are actually taking place.

We can begin by simply keeping a watchful eye on our reactions and responses to different situations and writing down what happens. In the process of observation we can dig a little more deeply, perhaps uncovering hidden motives and agendas, deeper fears masquerading as strengths, or personal desires expressed beneath our generosity. Using the moment of recall, as we write, we can look back at ourselves and our behaviour. Through such observation we get to know our secret selves and all the manifold parts of our being. The ways we subtly manipulate or emotionally bribe, how our needs can overshadow, how the ego so easily gains control.

Each day simply take a few minutes to observe quietly, to ponder, to write, to see what needs embracing and what needs letting go. We should do this with the attitude of being a friend to ourselves – not judging, punishing or putting down. Just being with whatever arises, accepting whatever comes as an opportunity to go deeper, but not to create further pain through condemnation or guilt. Suggestions for writing a journal can be found on the following page.

We can also use writing to have a dialogue with ourselves. Perhaps we are becoming aware of aspects of our being that are lost, or have been left behind and now feel cold and out of touch – parts that have not been acknowledged or loved. There may be a part of us that was hurt or abused when we were children, was rejected as a teenager, felt abandoned when our parents got divorced, or was not understood and therefore dismissed as unimportant. Now this part is sabotaging our relationships due to an insecurity, inability to commit, or fear of being hurt again. If we connect with this lost part of our being and find feelings of pain or hurt, then we can take the time in writing our journal to develop a dialogue, to give this part of us a chance to speak, to be heard, and therefore to be healed.

I was raped when I was six years old. Ever since then, all my adult life I have blamed myself for agreeing to go with the man who raped me, even though I knew I shouldn't. As if the whole event was therefore my fault. This has held me back from commitment in relationship, from being able to love fully or be trusting of a man. Through developing a dialogue with myself as a six-year-old I have been able to hear my child's story, the one that was filled with fear and not knowing what to do and not wanting to go in the car but terrified of doing the wrong thing. The little girl inside me had a chance to talk it out and actually be heard. No one had ever listened before. No one had taken time to hear her story. I have stopped blaming my child now. Instead I have had to acknowledge the real anger, the real pain of abuse. Now my healing can begin.

GRACE FLEMING

Keeping a journal teaches us how to hear the voice within, really to hear what we are feeling, or what different parts of our being may be saying to us. Beneath the conflict, the 'still, small voice' within speaks when we listen without judgement or resistance. That voice is our voice of wisdom, our all-knowing self. Listen carefully if you hear it speak. It may sound irrational, illogical or unfamiliar, but it will feel right deep inside.

TIME OUT: Suggestions for Writing a Journal

Choose a time when you are alone and quiet. Gently enter into a relaxed and quiet space by watching the incoming and outgoing breath for a few minutes.

When you are ready, begin to focus on a particular issue, a personal relationship or an aspect of yourself that you feel needs healing. Let the issue fill your being. Then write whatever you would like to say, be it words of anger, forgiveness, regret or love. Let the words come. Take your

---

time. When you have completed your piece, take a pause and consciously breathe for a few minutes.

You now become the writer but not the speaker. Listen rather than talk. Let the quiet, inner part of your being say to you whatever it may need to. Write down whatever comes to you, and in this way begin a dialogue. Ask questions and let the deeper part of you answer them. Remember to breathe. Let the dialogue evolve and grow as you share past memories, maybe re-experiencing them through the eyes of the person you were, rather than through your present eyes. This is a way of sorting out unresolved or repressed conflicts. Normally we spend our time in external communication and relationship, so this enables us to develop an internal relationship.

A journal is also a way of confronting ourselves and checking in to see where we are at. You can start each new page with a sentence and then let your writing flow from there. For instance:

- What I would most like people to know about me is. . . .
- What I find hardest to talk about is. . . .
- What I need to work on most in myself is. . . .
- What I have learned about myself is. . . .
- The way I can best serve my relationship is by. . . .
- I can become a good friend by. . . .
- What I am committed to doing is. . . .

And so on. Keep writing. Then take a pause and look back at what you have written. Do the same thing the following day or week and see if it has changed. Remember that the purpose is not just to release all the negative feelings (although that can be a great relief!) but to find your healing. To be real with yourself.

LETTING IN THE LOVE

To bring our relationships into a healthy and loving place involves being fearless and being able to surrender. We are fearless whenever we take a deep breath and allow ourselves to be intimate, when we confront that which is resisting closeness and we bring it into the light. Being able to surrender means not always having to be right or to be the victor – we can let go of control. It is a softening. Fearlessness and surrender are based on commitment, on a willingness to work through the issues. They keep us from getting stuck in ourselves or becoming too self-absorbed.

Making a commitment to a relationship does not necessarily mean we are committed to keeping the relationship going, regardless of how much we may suffer in the process. Knowing when to say goodbye is also an expression of being fearless and of surrendering. There are times when it is essential that we are honest with ourselves and ask why we are maintaining the relationship, especially if it is painful or abusive.

For the commitment is to a healthy communication, to allowing others to see who we are, to being intimate together, and to seeing and accepting others as they are. We are committing ourselves to sharing, to being honest and open, to supporting each other and to growing together. When one is wobbling the other is there to be a friend. It is a willingness to look at our own issues and how we are each affecting or influencing the relationship, and therefore it is a commitment to our own growth.

For us, our commitment to the spiritual journey was our common ground. It gave us the strength and wisdom to grow together, to learn and accept each other for who we are with all of our different moods, thoughts and feelings. As a couple the mirroring, the confronting and the loving is constantly challenging! We have to be honest about when the commitment is breaking down or being tested. We look at it, face it, deal with it, embrace it. Our relationship is a commitment to making friends with ourselves and to being a friend to each other.

EDDIE

There are bound to be times when any relationship gets rocky. These are actually the times when great progress can be made, as they highlight the areas that most need attention. However, this is also the time that it is most easy to walk away. The bottom line, therefore, has to be: do you really want this relationship to work? When you know the answer to this, then you will know if the relationship can be healed and what needs to be done, or if you can love this person better by being apart.

It is important to look at each one of our personal relationships in this light, whether with our partners, parents, children or friends. Difficulties *can* be healed if we choose to forgive, to communicate, to be open to listening and sharing, if we are willing to work with ourselves. When we allow difficulties between us to continue, causing hurt, pain, coldness and separation, then we are not being true to our healing. We are giving in to ego and personal desire rather than letting the heart speak. Even if the other person finds it difficult to communicate with us, we can at least make it known that we care, that we are available, that we do want to heal and to be friends. For the ultimate commitment we make is to our own peace. It is to finding the wholeness that is our birthright.

Each relationship is unique, working out its own parameters and values, respectful of the needs of each partner. Compromise may be necessary to accommodate all the differences, but this can be a creative endeavour rather than a resentful one. When we make friends with ourselves it is a delight to explore and make friends with another. Always there will be a challenge, that which pushes us beyond our normal limitations; in this way the relationship does not become stagnant.

I feel enormously privileged in having a remarkable woman to share my life with, who daily shows me what love means as she challenges me to be more myself. She seldom colludes with my weak spots or allows me to compromise or to ignore the values and principles that I am striving for. Thus, while not always comfortable in a traditional sense, our relationship allows both of us to grow. Love requests us to stay awake — to listen to it in the many guises and appearances in which it manifests. Sometimes it just asks us to surrender, to give up trying so hard and forcing things.

131

On other occasions, love whispers to us that action is needed. Compassionate and thoughtful action. And generally when we least like it. I have discovered that in the process of consciously choosing to be loving when I've felt exactly the opposite, my heart has spontaneously begun to open.

SERGE BEDDINGTON-BEHRENS

Healthy relationships are about letting the love come in and fill our being with joy, wonder, excitement, magic, caring and tenderness. About seeing what is right rather than focusing on what is wrong, about being patient and embracing the hard times. There is a spaciousness for each of us to be who we are, a nourishment of the deepest parts of our soul, a freedom to explore and share. A relationship that works is fun, playful and alive. It encourages and supports us to be who we really are, to take risks and enter into new areas both within ourselves and together.

Maintaining our own integrity in relationship is essential. Without it, dependency builds while insecurity grows. Feeling supported, encouraged to follow our own inclinations and to explore our own potential are aspects of a strong relationship. Then we have the space to be friends as well as lovers, to be side by side rather than one always ahead of the other – to be true partners.

PRACTICE – Communication Exercises

These exercises are to be done by two people together. Sit opposite each other, either on the floor or on chairs. Make sure you are close enough to each other to hold hands without stretching. You do not have to do both exercises, and if you do you can reverse their order if you wish.

Awareness of Content
In this exercise you sit opposite each other but you do not have to hold hands unless you want to. Have your eyes open. One of you will be talking, the other listening. You

132

can do this for as short or long a time as you want (we suggest ten minutes each to start with). It is helpful to time yourselves, so that you know when to stop.

(If you are doing this to solve communication problems, give enough time for both partners to talk before there is any feedback. Use the feedback time to work constructively with the issues that have been raised, not to criticize each other or defend yourself.)

Decide who goes first. The one who will be listening must remember just to listen. No feedback, nodding or shaking of the head, no thinking about other things. Just listen with an open heart. The one who is talking does not have to talk the whole time, non-stop. Let the words come from your heart, not just your head. Give them time to arise from within.

If you are the one who is talking first, start by talking for approximately ten minutes about your weak areas: how you make mistakes, how you don't always get it right. Dig deep inside and be as honest as you can. Take your time. Acknowledging yourself as you are is a major part of healing. Talk as freely and as openly as you can about your weak areas, those places where you are not as clear or as compassionate as you would like to be, those places you would like to heal. If you are the one who is listening, just listen.

At the end of your allotted time, reverse roles. The one who was listening now talk about yourself in the same way. And the one who was talking, just listen. At the end of the agreed time period, you can feed back to each other for a few minutes.

Then the partner who talked first starts again, this time to talk about your strengths, the things you do get right, the places inside you that are strong, wise, loving, gentle, compassionate. Be as honest here as you can. It is just as important to acknowledge your attributes, to feel these positive qualities and to know all sides of yourself.

After the allotted time, change over. After that, you can talk together freely.

Then repeat this process one more time, but on this occasion talk about what you would like to change within yourself and what you are going to do to bring this change into action. By the end of the session, make a commitment to yourself to do at least one thing to bring more healing into your life. It should be something you can begin now – in other words, not beyond your reach, but workable and realizable. Share this commitment with each other. Then begin it!

Awareness of Essence
In this exercise you sit opposite and hold each other's hands. Your eyes are closed throughout the practice. Spend a few minutes just breathing gently and relaxing. Let go of any tension that arises from sitting in this way. Just become present. Breathe into your belly – soft belly. Take fifteen–twenty minutes to do this exercise.

Now, through your hands, become aware of the person opposite you. Become aware of the fact that they are a physical person just like you, that they have flesh, bones, blood, organs, toes, fingers, eyes, hair. In your mind, see this other person's body. The outer form may look a little different from yours, but notice how the ingredients are basically the same. Become aware of your body and the body opposite you and notice how small the differences are, yet how great the similarities.

Then become aware that this person too has thoughts and feelings like yours. These thoughts and feelings can motivate and give purpose; they can also overwhelm or confuse. Notice that this person, like you, makes mistakes. That they don't always get things right. Like you, they are attempting to live this life the best they can, but sometimes they are not sensitive enough. They might get angry a little too often, they get hurt or rejected, they wobble and feel insecure and then lash out. Like you, they have weak areas. Silently become aware of your own weaknesses and see how the two of you are really very similar – two human beings trying to make it work in this world.

But this human being opposite you does not just have weak areas. They also have great strengths and attributes. Like you do. They love deeply, they care for others, they want to help, they have great endurance and inner fortitude. They work hard to get things right. Deep within them is compassion and kindness and gentleness. Just as there is within you. Silently feel and acknowledge the strengths and love you both have.

Now become aware that this being is not just a physical being with thoughts and feelings, but there is also a great spirit present. Within the being opposite you, as within you, is a tremendous energy, a bright light that shines. This is not limited to name and form, to colour, race, creed, age or personality. It is unlimited, nameless, formless, colourless, raceless, creedless, ageless, free of identity. It is pure essence, that which is in each one of us. Through your hands feel the warmth of this great spirit, of this light shining.

When you are ready, you can open your eyes and look at this light. Let it shine through you and meet the light in front of you.

7

OURSELVES, OUR PLANET

If you can, help others; if you cannot do that,
at least do not harm them.

THE DALAI LAMA

If we are to heal our relationships with each other then we also have to include healing our relationship with the earth, as this primary relationship sustains all others. And we are slowly discovering just how one-sided and abusive this relationship has been. We are learning about the hole in the ozone layer, how the oceans are polluted, about the greenhouse effect and global warming, about the slaughter of the whales and the dolphins, about the destruction of the rain forests and about the misuse of natural resources.

Ignoring the needs of the earth is a reflection of our ignoring ourselves – it shows a lack of sufficient care for ourselves and each other. Conversely, when we care for the earth we are expressing our care for ourselves and our children. It is to be responsible for our lives. If we are to live, then so too must our world – they cannot be separated. That is why the Native Americans do not think only of their own lives: everything they do is for the generation to come seven generations beyond them. That way their world is kept alive, vibrant and healthy, so seven generations ahead can be healthy. Can we say this of the world we are now creating? Are we asleep to the whispers of eternity? In *The Way Ahead* Václav Havel, President of the Czech Republic, recalls:

> As a boy, I lived for some time in the country and I clearly remember an experience from those days: I used to walk to school in a nearby village along a cart track through the fields and, on the way, see a huge smokestack of some hurriedly built factory. It spewed dense brown smoke and scattered it across the sky. Each time I saw it, I had an intense sense of something profoundly wrong, of humans soiling the heavens.

We cannot isolate our own healing from that of the planet as a whole, cannot see our own life as different from the life of the plants, animals, each other or the earth. The earth is a living organism like us: the rocks are its bones, the soil is its flesh, the great oceans, lakes and rivers are its blood. The human species is an integral part of creation, and is absolutely crucial for the survival of the whole. For unlike other life forms we have the great responsibility of being the caretakers of every life on this planet. Dependent on each one of us is the future of us all. In *The Way Ahead* Helen Caldicott, the Nobel Peace Prize recipient for Physicians for Social Responsibility, explains:

> Mankind has a huge brain that has developed very fast in evolutionary terms and which enables us to make and hold on to things like guns. In this way we dominate the earth. . . . We think nature was put there purely for our convenience because it says in Genesis that man was given domination over the earth. But who wrote Genesis? Did the koalas write Genesis? Did the elephants write Genesis?

We have within our grasp the power to do great good, to make our lives purposeful and meaningful. Let us see how we can give rather than just take, contribute rather than just consume. We do not need to dominate or destroy in order to survive —

rather, let us be guardians protecting the lives that are in our care. We have the potential for a saner and more harmonious world. If we see separation, then we believe we can hurt the earth but do not hurt ourselves; but if we see the interconnectedness of all things then we know that the life of a single butterfly is as important as our own.

Thankfully, more and more people are realizing that a change is needed and that this change is to do with the collective consciousness of the whole. The focus has to shift in consciousness from 'me' to 'other'. When we value each other as ourselves, then the need to put 'me' first begins to dissolve and we open to a multi-dimensional view of life. There is an awareness of our place among others in the human family, and of our place as humans on this earth. We are mere children, and this planet is far older than humankind. Can we not respect the earth and all the species that live on and with her? They have been here far longer than we have, and they will still be here long after we have gone. As the biologist Rupert Sheldrake describes in *The Way Ahead*:

> If everyone in England died tomorrow, in ten years' time London would be green all over. There would be grass growing up through the streets, there would be trees in the gardens. There would be crumbling buildings covered with ivy and other plants growing on top of them.

WHEN WE HEAR THE WORLD CRY

To live in the world as responsible human beings means to live as the solution, not to dwell on the problem. Honouring what others have done is important if it acts as an inspiration, but let us not leave the action to others and then blame them if things go wrong. Is it not time to take charge of our own future?

When we do not cooperate, even in a small way, then we are contributing to the devastation of a great and beautiful world. For how lucky we are to be alive! To breathe the air, to smell the flowers, to swim in the oceans, to climb the mountains, to enjoy the raindrops! The earth sustains us all without question. If each one of us gave as much as we are given, what a joyous place this would be!

Perhaps I had the making of a mystic while still a teenager, as I regularly used to get up at dawn and cycle out of the city to the woods and sit there for an hour or so listening to the natural world awakening. Or I would go to a spinney at twilight and sit there wrapped in a blanket, imbibing the quiet spirit of the woods long into the dark. One day I came to my favourite spinney to find it half-destroyed by bulldozers grubbing up the landscape for a housing estate. I could see the life-force of the spinney ebbing away. I was shocked to my depths. In anguish, my stricken soul cried out to the trees in sorrow for this desecration. Then anger for all the worldly injustices boiled over and with a handy pick I buried the workmen's tools and clothing. And from then on I became a nature activist, doing whatever I could to foil developers from despoiling nature.

MUZ MURRAY

The abuse of the planet can easily overwhelm and render us numb, angry, or even crazy. It reflects the pain of humanity – the pain of not communicating, caring or loving one another. How do we live with this pain, feeling the acid rain, knowing the rain forests are being destroyed or seeing the oceans polluted? How can we pay attention to the state of the world and not lose our sanity or even our humanity? How do we stay involved and not allow the fear to make us indifferent? What does it take to make us less self-obsessed and more altruistically involved?

I had been an accountant and an estate agent and had suffered a thrombosis. Finally I realized it was time to change my life. So I learned relaxation, de-stressed and improved my lifestyle. But the real shift took place when I got a job with Greenpeace. Going to sea and watching volunteers risk their lives by putting their bodies between the whales and the harpoons. The pain of saving the whales and the seals was so enormous. It opened my heart completely. It was a commitment to something much bigger than me personally, it took me beyond my limitations. I still felt a coward

139

inside – I was really seasick on the Rainbow Warrior *and got very scared when I was sent to Iceland to get information for the campaign. But I saw how we can collectively make a difference when we stopped the seal culling in the Orkneys.*

MALCOLM STERN

Perhaps it is through personally experiencing the life force that pulsates in every cell, linking us inevitably and intimately together, that we recognize how the pain of the world is also our pain; that in our healing lies the healing of the world. We do not feel compassion without having felt pain. And this is what healing is: the embracing of our pain with compassion. When we feel the suffering in the world, then we are experiencing our connectedness.

The Vietnamese monk, Thich Nhat Hanh, says 'To hear within ourselves the sounds of the earth crying.' When we open to the earth's pain we open to our own woundedness. Healing is an owning of our own wounds. When we hear the earth crying, when we are able to own the truth of that, then we do not need to apologize for the tears we shed. We are experiencing the profound interconnectedness of all life. In *The Way Ahead*, the environmentalist Jonathon Porritt explains how the healing of ourselves and the earth are so intertwined:

> Ecology is a process of healing, a way of providing meaning in an otherwise sterile and empty world. . . . It is the wisdom of ecology that reinstructs us now about the importance of balance and the inter-relatedness of all living things on earth. And it is the wisdom of religion that allows us to transcend our material confines and maintain contact with the source of meaning itself. . . . Then we can go out and take action to put things right, inspired by that vision. It lies, quite simply, in learning to sing again the song of the Earth, and singing it again and again and again until we all sing in harmony.

And then we are able to come forth and speak up. To take responsibility for our place in the whole. How often do we walk along the beach or in a city park and see rubbish tossed

140

carelessly on the ground? Do we pick it up and put it in a rubbish bin? Or do we leave it for someone else to clean up? Do we walk past, wondering what foolish person did such a thing? Or do we even notice it at all? We may think that individually we don't make a difference, but every action adds to the whole and makes for a kinder and saner world. As the pacifist Indian leader Mahatma Gandhi said: 'Almost anything you do will seem insignificant, but it is very important that you do it.'

In the early 1970s I was teaching vegetarian cookery. Someone asked me why I was bothering to do this, as surely it would not make any difference to the amount of animals being killed or the way they were treated. I didn't know a logical answer. I just knew that I was contributing what I could. I said that if I teach two people and they pass it on, then that can make four, and they can tell eight, and so it grows exponentially. Little did I realize that twenty years later England would have the highest number of vegetarians per capita of any Western country! It's not as if we all have to become vegetarian, but it does show that we can all make a difference, each in our own small way, by just doing what we feel is right, what we know in our hearts.

DEBBIE

HOW CAN I SERVE?

We can no longer live in isolation, focusing only on our own survival and ignoring that of others. It is not our world alone – it belongs to each of us equally. How can we give only to ourselves? As we open our heart to others, service becomes the expression of our love, our caring for all beings. There is a natural spilling over that takes place, a quiet urge to give, to share, to help. In *How Can I Help?* the spiritual teacher Ram Dass suggests that:

Service . . . is a vehicle through which we reach a deeper understanding of life. Each step we take, each moment in which we grow towards a greater understanding of unity, steadily transforms us into instruments of that help which

141

truly heals. . . . It all seems natural and appropriate. You live, you help. . . . Yet if we stop to consider why it all felt so good, we sense that some deeper process was at work. Expressing our innate generosity, we experienced our 'kin'-ship, our 'kind'-ness. It was 'us'. In service, we taste unity.

There are so many ways we can give. A simple smile can be as important as food or clothing. Have you ever walked down the street and looked at the faces passing you by? And have you seen how few people are smiling – that most of them are looking so glum? Just for one day, try smiling at the people you pass! Not a phoney grin but a genuine, caring, warm smile. And see how much joy you can bring, how people's faces can light up. Wherever you are – on a bus, train, in a shop, at work – feel a love for those around you, a silent warmth and acceptance. And see what a difference it can make. Mother Teresa reminds us:

> We may wonder: Whom can I love and serve? Where is the face of God to whom I can pray? The answer is simple: that hungry one, that naked one, that lonely one, that unwanted one, is my brother and my sister. If we have no peace, it is because we have forgotten that we belong to each other.

As a start, try spending one whole day thinking selflessly – thinking not of yourself, but of others and their needs. Every time you start focusing on what you want or what you would like, stop, and then see what someone else might want or how you could help. Even try doing this for a few days! It might seem like a long time, but it is an excellent way of reckoning with yourself, of seeing how much you can really give where you may not have previously realized.

Maybe your local hospital needs volunteer visitors. Or the shelter for the homeless needs someone to collect clothing. Or your elderly neighbours need some help with their shopping. Maybe you could organize the recycling of your office waste. Perhaps a colleague could use a lift home, a child needs babysitting, or the man on the street corner is hungry for a hot meal. There are refugee children in need of support; trees to be saved from the axe, trees to be planted, nature reserves to be maintained. See what you can contribute to help others feel good and to bring healing to the world.

> *When we lived in Boulder, Colorado, we would walk through the back lanes, enjoying the great variety of gardens, the abundant flowers and vegetables growing there. But one backyard was filled with old bicycles, hundreds of them, stacked in rows. We discovered that the man who lived there had a bicycle shop in town and collected all these old, discarded bikes. Then, in his own time, he would rebuild them until they were working perfectly. He would then send truckloads of these bikes up to an Indian reservation in Wyoming. It was a very poor reservation – few of the people there had transport. His objective was 1,800 bikes, enough to ensure that everyone had a bicycle they could get around on.*
>
> EDDIE

These are simple ways to help; obviously there are much bigger ones too. In order to serve we need the faith that we can heal, that our relationships and the planet can heal. Faith gives us the courage to embrace our pain: it ignites a strong and powerful energy that gives us the will to keep going through all situations.

The faith we are talking about here is born through developing a relationship with ourselves. It is not an external faith or belief that something or someone outside will heal us or do it for us. That is not our objective. Here we are talking about drawing faith from deep within. To feel our whole being involved, touching every cell of our body, mind and heart. Consciously to bring our attention inward and to awaken the energy that is required to take us beyond our separate selves to the place where we all meet. Why do we resist? What is it that holds us back from coming together in ways that can help each other and the planet? What stops us from asking, 'How can I serve?'

*In the mid-1970s a man who had conquered a severe drinking
problem contacted me, saying that we must establish a residential
centre for yoga and rehabilitation. I told him this was a crazy idea;
we had absolutely no money or backers. But he persisted. And
suddenly I knew we had to start this centre and that my protests
about the absence of money, while absolutely true, were also really
irrelevant. From that moment on I had no doubt that we would
succeed. Ten months later we opened our centre in a country
mansion set in beautiful grounds! Now, some sixteen years later,
we are firmly established: we are a second home to thousands of
people – fit and unfit, well and sick.*

HOWARD KENT

Rather than being immersed in and overwhelmed by what is
wrong, we can focus on how we can contribute to what is right.
By working with ourselves in each moment, we help; by caring
for each other, we help; by seeing the unity in diversity, we
help. Faith gives us added strength that we may not have had
before; it sustains us in all situations, even when we wonder
what we are doing. It is the faith that the earth will not crumble
or the heavens fall; it is the faith that we can be whole. That
what we individually do *is* of importance. It is a feeling that
takes us beyond our limitations, beyond what we think we are
capable of. Faith takes us to places we never thought we could
go.

*I was in Oklahoma, driving back to where I was staying after a
day's teaching, when my car suddenly stopped. As I was on a hill
and there was no way of restarting the car, I simply rolled back
down the hill and into the driveway of a church. There were plenty
of cars around, so I presumed someone would be able to help me.
As I walked into the church I found myself in the midst of a huge
Afro-American wedding! It was a wonderful sight. And despite
being dressed in tuxedos, within minutes five young guys were
under the bonnet, trying to figure out what was wrong with the
car. I was very touched by their willingness to help, but nothing
seemed to be working.*

*Suddenly we heard shouting from the other side of the road. I
looked up to see a woman in a dressing gown, clinging to the far*

144

side of a big fence. She was screaming for help. As we all stood, stunned and wondering what to do, two men came out of the building behind her, dressed in white doctor's coats. They put her in a straitjacket and led her away. The next minute my car had started again without anyone having made any major adjustments to it!

The following day I recounted these events to the participants of the workshop I was teaching. One of the men told me that this place was a home for the mentally disabled, and that it was actually run by a friend of his. He explained how he had been planning to bring alternative therapists to the home, but he had been procrastinating and delaying for months. He went on to say, 'What you have just told me has convinced me to start treatments there immediately. I believe that woman crying out for help at the moment that you were stopped there is a message that I needed to hear. She has given me the faith to help.'

DEBBIE

RESPECTING OUR HUMANITY

Our life on earth is going through great change. Alongside the abuse of the planet is the upheaval and removal of old structures: the Berlin Wall has come down, the Eastern bloc no longer exists. It is happening so fast that we can no longer draw an accurate map. Technology is advancing beyond our imagination. Traditional religions are redefining their roles and teachings; many of the old forms are disintegrating and new directions are emerging. There is tremendous change all around us.

Just a few days after President Yeltsin had stopped the governmental uprising in October 1993, a Russian naval ship came on a courtesy call to Dartmouth, the town where we live in Devon. It was the first Russian visit in seventy-five years. This huge grey warship berthed in the river between the yachts and fishing boats. The next day the town was filled with Russian sailors taking photos, buying postcards, shampoo, shoes, cigarettes, chocolate. In the supermarket I saw three sailors staring open-mouthed at the

145

shelves laden with food. My mind was filled with television images
of Russian shops with empty shelves and queues of hungry people.
My eyes met those of one young sailor. His were filled with
amazement at the abundance, while mine were filled with sadness
that we have so much while others have so little. The townspeople
were able to go on board the boat, to walk the long decks that only a
short while ago would have been considered enemy territory.

DEBBIE

The survival of humanity is, however, not just a matter of dismantling borders or countries, changing politics, providing more food or planting more trees. Answers to the world's difficulties are not so simply resolved. These things are import-ant and obviously help; but until we go deeper, into the root cause of the problems, then such actions can be like bandages, hiding the real wound beneath. For our streets are full of homeless people, the prisons are overflowing, and countries are at war with themselves and each other. To bring lasting and effective change we have to focus on changing attitudes; on changing the fundamental ways we think deep, deep down in ourselves. In the foreword to *The Way Ahead* the actor and human rights activist Richard Gere says:

As we enter the precarious new century and millennium we, as
custodians of this planet, find ourselves at the unpleasant end of a
botched experiment. True happiness still eludes us and now our
very survival depends on our ability and determination to utterly
change our ways – politically, economically, spiritually.

The attitudes in need of change are those of greed, hatred, prejudice, fear and delusion – primal attitudes connected to self-survival at any cost, regardless of the destruction that may be caused in the process. They arise in every relationship between ourselves and another. Moments when we are unable to surrender the ego, when we lash out and hurt each other, when our craving overcomes our sensibility, when we take more than we give or when we blame another's colour or religion for our own ignorance. Until we each, individually, see that our survival is inevitably connected to the survival of all,

146

we will continue to hurt each other and to abuse the world around us.

We are all intimately involved. We breathe the same air, walk the same earth. No one is insignificant, no head is higher than the next person's. The only place we find a difference is in the human mind, which is where the separations take place. If we were blind we could not see the colour of a person's skin, so it would make no difference; if we were deaf, we would not hear the insults. If there was an effort by each one of us to create less pain, if everyone in the whole world just stopped for one minute to pray for peace, what a revolution that would bring about!

Satish Kumar was travelling on foot through Russia on a peace walk. In his book *No Destination*, he describes how in Armenia they were invited to give a talk at a tea factory. There he saw for himself how the simplest of gestures can make our world a kinder place to live in:

One of the women who had invited us into the factory stood up and rushed out of the room. Moments later she came back with four packets of tea. She said to us, 'What you are saying, I fully agree with – every word. Here are four packets of tea made in our factory. I know you are walking and you want to travel light, but these packets are very important. Please carry them with you. They are not for you. Please give one to our Premier in Moscow, one to the President of France, one to the Prime Minister of England and one to the President of the United States of America. Tell them that if they get mad in their minds and think of pushing the button to drop nuclear bombs, they should stop for a moment and have a fresh cup of tea from these packets. That will give them a chance to remember that the simple people of the world want bread not bombs, want life not death.'

PRACTISING HARMLESSNESS

In Sanskrit, the ancient language in which various Eastern philosophical texts were written, there is a word *ahimsa*, which means harmlessness. The Eastern teachings urge us to practise

147

harmlessness with both ourselves and others. This is an extraordinary teaching as it uncovers the often subtle ways in which we are actually creating harm, usually without realizing it. By getting emotionally upset we hurt another's feelings, through disrespect or denial we cause psychological harm, by taking more than we need we cause someone else to go without, by buying products made with cheap labour we support the exploitation of those workers.

To practise harmlessness properly is a unique experience. It sounds simple, but it is not always so easy. It means developing respect for all life. It involves questioning each area of ourselves. How do we deal with a partner who does not respect our feelings? How do we heal self-destructive or self-denigrating thought patterns? What do we do when ants invade the kitchen, or slugs eat our carefully planted vegetables?

To be truly harmless demands a genuine and honest approach to each situation we face. In this way, compassion and loving-kindness can become active moment to moment, integrated into our lives. In every situation we can choose the more humane approach: with the food we eat, the clothes we wear, our use of the earth's resources, our communication with each other, our relationship to all humankind. Combined with faith, *ahimsa* gives us the strength to do what we know is right.

I was born in 1919, when the world was slowly trying to right itself from the incredible carnage of the First World War. When my elder brother went to public school he joined the Officers' Training Corps and proudly paraded around in his uniform. When my turn came to go to the same school I knew that I could not follow in his footsteps. This resulted in an interview with the headmaster. Fortunately he was understanding in my right to conscientiously object. It may be argued that I was just a product of my times, but all the others of my age joined in the war games. Something in my young mind had flared up to say, 'No!'

Later, in the 1930s, I learned of Gandhi and his teaching on ahimsa, *the absence of violence. This, I realized, was already deep within me. Then, in 1939, when war came, I was accepted as a conscientious objector. Thankfully I learned that cowardice did not lie behind my views as during the bombing of London I helped run a centre for the bombed-out and, from time to time, had to cycle through the streets during the height of the raids with shrapnel coming down like hail. Now I can see how, some sixty-five years ago, my beliefs marked me for life. To me* ahimsa *is more important than all the words of the scriptures, for it is an experience beyond understanding.*

HOWARD KENT

We sat watching the evening news on television. One disaster after another – killings, war, famine, strikes. Then, unexpectedly, there was a peace gathering in South Africa. Offices closed and the workers all came out in the streets, holding hands. Thousands upon thousands singing together, sweetly lifting their voices to bring peace. And for the first time in a long time no one was killed that night. The power of people gathering in the name of peace is very great. The faith that peace can work. It can transform fear into fearlessness, hate into love, harm into harmlessness, separation into unity, ignorance into wisdom.

EDDIE

TIME OUT: To Look at Harmlessness

Take some time to look at your relationship to harmlessness and how you may be causing harm without even realizing it, perhaps simply by not honouring or respecting yourself or your world. Use this time to look at your behaviour, your underlying motives and attitudes, and at what you can do to bring more caring and respect into your life. Have a paper and pen to write down whatever comes to you.

- Are there areas in my life that are causing harm to myself or to anyone else?
- How can I start to treat myself with more acceptance and love?
- How can I be more respectful of myself?

149

- Does practising harmlessness mean ending an abusive relationship?
- Does it mean communicating with someone I do not talk to any more?
- Or forgiving someone, even if I choose not to talk to them?
- Do I need to find a less stressful job or a quieter place to live?
- Does it mean respecting my environment more?
- What can I do to be more useful to the world?
- How can I be a more loving caretaker?
- What one contribution can I make in the next week towards the healing of the planet?

Take time to look inside and ask yourself these questions. See where in your life you may not be respecting your precious humanness, but dismissing yourself and your feelings as unimportant. Then apply the same insight to the way you treat others and see where you can be more harmless. Perhaps you can speak more gently, get angry less often, or touch and hold and caress a little more.

HONOURING THE EARTH

Nature constantly proves to be greater than the destruction we impose. The beauty of a sunset, the turn of a leaf, the meeting of a wild creature's eyes with our own, all fill our heart. Eddie was swimming one morning in the sea when he lifted his head and saw a seal swimming alongside him. The seal looked just as curious to see him as he was to see the seal. Such images stir within us a response often forgotten and easily ignored. We hear of a dolphin coming to the rescue of a drowning swimmer, or of plants that have been found to help cure ailments, yet we do not acknowledge our place in nature as a co-species on this earth. Perhaps it is because nature is still a mystery, beyond our limited comprehension. Even to begin to understand, we have to become quiet and surrendered. How does the yolk get inside the egg shell? Where do the brilliant colours come from that the peacock displays, or the sweet smell of a rose?

The awe that fills us when we open ourselves to seeing life in all its beauty and impermanence is the awe of the miracle of creation, the extraordinary reality that an oak tree grows out of an acorn, a frog out of a slimy mass of frogspawn. Many call this miracle the divine, others call it the life force, or universal consciousness. The name does not matter. The experience of the presence of this force is what moves us, what takes us into other realms and beliefs.

I was about nineteen years old and I was returning my car to its normal parking spot under the old oak tree when I became transfixed by the tree itself; for although I had seen it thousands of times before, now I seemed to be looking at it as if for the first time. For some reason I noticed how unique and individual this particular tree was, and just how beautiful. But more than that, this time I had a flash of understanding: the tree was unique because it expressed the Divine. This was the advent of my recognition that everything in existence is an incarnation of God.

JUSTIN CARSON

As our healing is intimately connected to the healing of the planet, it is wise to spend time in nature and allow the beauty and power of the earth to calm our nerves, ease our thoughts and relax our bodies. To take time to walk. To sit gently at the foot of a great tree and close our eyes. To feel the water of a stream, river or the sea washing over our bodies, cooling our minds. Even in the midst of cities there are parks filled with birdsong and flowers that can refresh our being, that remind us of our purpose and healing. We can see beauty in the rain and wind as much as in sunlight, we can honour the trees that give us shelter and the insects that help keep the balance of nature.

Try spending a few minutes being completely quiet and still in a natural setting, whether by the sea, in a wood or a garden, or beside a stream. Let yourself surrender to your environment. As you do, feel the energy around you, the force of life pulsating, the gentleness of life embracing. Let the elements caress you, soothe you, heal you. For you are a part of the elements, a part of nature. It is there to bring you to wholeness.

When the earth speaks to us, through the many creatures and plants that live on it, then we know our interconnectedness deep inside. There is a respect and reverence for the great gift of life we have been given, for the sacredness and divinity that are in every moment.

The inauguration of the Holy Isle in Scotland was a truly holy day. Holy Isle had recently been bought by Samye Ling, a Tibetan Buddhist monastery near Lockerbie to build an ecumenical retreat centre. On this particular day we were all gathering to celebrate Samye Ling officially taking ownership. Eddie and I had been invited to attend. Leaving the monastery early in the morning, we drove to the west coast and took the ferry to Arran. It was a cold, grey day in April, with the wind blowing fiercely. The boat ride was followed by a bumpy bus ride down the coast of Arran, carefully avoiding stray sheep wandering across the road, and descending a steep hill to a small rocky beach. Here we all gathered to await the fishermen to ferry us across to the Holy Isle lying just offshore.

It was a wonderfully diverse group that gathered there. The abbot of Samye Ling, Akong Rinpoche, was dressed in flowing brocade robes of red and gold, while other Tibetan Buddhists were in maroon robes; beside them were bishops and monks of various Christian orders representing the Churches of Scotland, some in flowing black, others in long white or red robes. All were wearing scarves or hats and long overcoats to protect them against the cold wind. There were a collection of newspaper reporters, women in skirts and high heels, as well as a few older women in tweed jackets and boots. Lord and Lady Ennals had come, and the Scottish MP, David Steel and his wife. Alongside them were a motley collection of duffel coat wearers with brightly coloured woollen hats.

(As we waited in the cold, I quietly wished that walking on water had been more popular in America than learning how to walk on fire. Walking on hot coals would be no help now, whereas being able to walk on water would mean we wouldn't have to be waiting here, bundled against the wind. Far more practical!)

However, when the boat arrived it was worth the wait. It was like a cattle truck – a concrete slab with iron railings around the edge. But the ramp could not get as close as it would have liked to the quay, so between us on the beach and the boat in the sea lay a stretch of icy-cold water, too far to jump, but just shallow enough to wade through. We stood at the back and watched the Tibetan lamas, the bishops, the reporters, the tweeded ones and the duffel coats all hoist their attire and make their way through this very cold water to reach the boat. Except for one elderly lady who decided she was not going to get her feet wet and leaped high and long, as if she could fly, to be caught in the ferryman's arms. It was a sight for sore eyes – a true initiation!

Reaching Holy Isle we all walked (with squelching wet feet), serenaded by bagpipes, to a cave that had been used by monks as a retreat for hundreds of years. The island had always been a holy place, a place of pilgrimage, although in recent years it had fallen out of use. Now the Buddhists plan to bring that sacredness back to life. On the muddy and slippery slopes outside the cave each of the dignitaries offered their words of praise and blessings to the place, acknowledging the site as sacred for people of all faiths. It was a humble and moving moment. The sun shone, and the gentle sound of a harp filled the air.

This was a true gathering of the spirit, a rejoicing in the discovery of a holy place and the bringing of it back to life. It was not just a religious ceremony, nor a collection of new-agers. This was a gathering to celebrate the open heart, a willingness of many different beliefs to participate, without the need for form or dogma. In the diversity of those gathered lay a unity of purpose and vision. It was heart-warming to see journalists, politicians and religious leaders come together in celebration of an event that was reported with dignity and respect. There was a recognition of the contribution that such a small island could make to the whole – a contribution of acceptance, tolerance, worship and devotion. Later that day, as we waited for the fishermen to ferry us off the island, we felt we had been present at a special moment in time, an expression of reverence for the earth and of humankind's unique relationship between the earth below, the spirit within and the heavens above. Although humankind has the power to destroy, it also has the power to heal, to bring to life, to respect and honour.

DEBBIE

153

PRACTICE – Harvesting the Gifts of Our Ancestors

You can do this practice standing up, actually walking backwards and then forwards; you can do it standing still in one place; or you can sit down. Have your eyes closed. For a few minutes just focus on your breathing, watching the breath come in and out. Become quieter. Take about half an hour to do this practice.

Starting from this present moment begin to move back in time . . . through the events and encounters of this day . . . this week . . . this month . . . this year. . . . Walk slowly back through the decades into your young adulthood . . . your adolescence . . . your childhood . . . soon you are a baby in your mother's arms . . . now back in her womb and returning to the climactic point of this life's conception.

But what lives in you did not begin then. . . . Walk back into your parents . . . into their lives . . . then back into the wombs that bore them . . . back into your grandparents.

Continue slowly back into and through the nineteenth century . . . into ancestors whose names you no longer know but whose gestures and smiles live on in you. . . . Keep moving back in this river of life . . . back through the Industrial Revolution . . . back into simpler, harsher times marked by the seasons . . . back into the Middle Ages.

Move back through times of plague and pilgrimage into the lives of ancestors with hands – like your hands – that chiselled the stones of great cathedrals . . . and eyes – like your eyes – that tracked the movement of the stars. . . . Keep going back to the dawning of the civilizations we know and enter the early, wandering times . . . the small bands in forest settlements, their feasts and rituals around the sacred fire, and their long marches through the ages of ice.

Back through the millennia you walk with them, to your beginnings in the heartland of Africa. . . . And now, with the very first ones, you stand at the edge of the forest. . . . Pause now, looking over the savannah. . . . The journey of your people lies ahead. . . . Walk forward on it now. . . . Retracing your steps, returning through time.

As you do so, each ancestor has a gift to bestow . . . open your arms and hands to receive it as you walk forward through the centuries. . . . They who passed on to you the texture of your skin, the shape of your back, the marrow in your bones . . . they also have courage to give you, and stubbornness and laughter. . . . These gifts are yours.

Gather them as you come forward through the years to this present moment, this brink in time. . . . They who loved and tended this earth give you the strength and wisdom you will need now, to do what must be done so that their journey may continue.

8

THE MAGIC
OF
MEDITATION

Without holding on to the past, anticipating the future
or interfering with the present,
let the mind settle naturally, of its own accord.
LAMA YESHE LOSAL

The journey to healing consists of connecting with ourselves, by getting in touch with our true feelings and embracing them into a wholeness. We are hindered in doing this primarily by the stress and demands of the physical world, for it acts like a magnet, drawing us in through our senses and desires. There is unending distraction! The most effective way to relieve and counterbalance such distraction is through relaxation and meditation, where the constant pressure of being drawn outwards is eased and we withdraw inwards, to the peace at the core of our being. In a truly relaxed or contemplative state we have the chance to listen to ourselves, to retreat into the essence of our existence, to connect with who we really are. What we find is simple and ordinary, yet it is filled with magic!

We usually think of magic as something that takes us out of the ordinary and creates something extraordinary – a moment or situation where the mundane no longer fits and goes beyond our normal reality. Ordinary magic is different. It appears when we recognize the miracle in the fact that we breathe, that we can taste, touch, smell, that our heart is beating, that the planet is in orbit. If the movement of the planet altered by one millisecond, none of us would be here. We don't even notice the planet moving, it is so ordinary. Is it not magic that it stays in such perfect orbit? To be alive, to feel the presence of our being standing on the ground in relationship to the earth, to the air, to the colour of the leaves and the way they move in the wind: this is magic.

As we simplify our lives and create the space to be still, receptive and peaceful, ordinary magic is revealed. Relaxing into the quiet without any resistance, we discover magic waiting for us. It is everywhere. It is in every action, every breath, every moment. Unassuming, like the flutter of a butterfly, the dew on a leaf, or a cool breeze on a warm day. The magic is the peace that is already within us, for it is our innate nature. Peace is not something we can get, for we already have it. Waking up to that peace, entering into a space of clarity and gentleness, is therefore ordinary, a return to our natural state of being. The worry, confusion and fear, this is the extraordinary. If we can let go of the 'extra', at least for a few minutes, then we enter into a quiet and peaceful space within.

PAYING ATTENTION

To do this we need to become observant and attentive to our thoughts and emotions: those that are repetitive and habitual, that react rather than respond. By paying attention to what is, we see beyond our own impression of how things are to seeing things in their own right, without any prejudice or preference, without our usual reference points. Just as it is. We see the extraordinary within the ordinary, the magic in the moment, the simplicity of life's complexities. The great Chinese philosopher Lao Tzu said, 'Those who of old were good practitioners of Tao [Way of Truth] did not use it to make the people bright, but rather used it to make them simple.'

There is a wonderful story about the Zen master Ikkyu. One day a man visited him and asked the master to write some words about the truth that would help him in his life. Ikkyu immediately wrote down the single word 'Attention'. The man was a little taken aback at so short a response, so he asked Ikkyu to add something more. The master picked up his pen and wrote 'Attention. Attention.' The man was now getting a little impatient, and irritably expressed his hope for something more profound or of greater length. Ikkyu again picked up his pen and this time he wrote 'Attention. Attention. Attention.' Finally, the frustrated man asked Ikkyu what this meant. Ikkyu responded by saying, 'Attention means attention.'

Our healing grows by paying attention. Being aware of our feelings, thoughts, actions, attitudes, habits and behaviour. Listening to our heart, to our inner voice, and honouring what we find. Becoming more conscious of ourselves in relationship to the whole, of our movements, of our presence. Paying attention means that we see more objectively, but without being self-centred. Just watching, noticing. Paying attention to the breath enables the mind to quieten. Then we pay attention to the thoughts and emotions that arise and pass through the mind, and we become a witness to the inner dialogue. When we are attentive to whatever it is we are doing, it is easier to focus and see clearly.

As a freestyle skier I lived for many years in the Rocky Mountains. This taught me the necessity of paying attention. If your mind drifts during meditation practice, you simply notice it drifting and bring your attention back to the practice again – no big deal. However, if your mind drifts while you are skiing, you can hit a tree!

EDDIE

Paying attention is learning about mindfulness, awareness and skilful means. To be mindful means to be present, simply to do what we are doing with full attention, whether we are washing the dishes, answering the telephone or sitting in meditation. To be aware means having the alertness of mind to see and be sensitive to all the things going on around us, whether it be another's needs or feelings, or our own reactions in each instance. Being skilful means having the ability to deal with situations without causing harm, to be able to say or do what is necessary without creating further pain. It is practising *ahimsa*. Being skilful is respecting ourselves and others – it is about not giving advice unless it is asked for. It is about handling ourselves with dignity and honesty in a world full of contradiction.

Practices such as deep relaxation and meditation are fundamental for developing mindfulness, awareness and skilful means. Through these practices we find our ground – they form the foundation from which we grow in understanding and compassion. Such practices enable a letting go of the inner stress, so that the mind comes into a quiet stillness and we can open the heart. We cannot complete the healing journey in the mind alone; we have to be able to go beyond the mind, the mental chatter and endless desires, and enter into the deeper levels of our being. Only then do we see ourselves clearly and release that which is keeping us bound.

Relaxation and meditation can become part of our daily routine to give us greater insight and compassion. We wear warm clothing in winter to protect ourselves from the cold weather, light clothing in the hot, summer months, rainwear in the rain. We use moisturizers to protect against dryness and screens against the sun. Now we can use another form of protection: the kind that protects us from suffering, from the weather of anger, guilt, shame and bitterness. We have learned how to defend ourselves from the climate, from the external forces of nature, but how about the inner climate? That which invades our health and well-being from the inside? The external storms are easy to see and detect. What we need is gentleness, kindness, openness and forgiveness to protect us from the storms inside our minds, and to take us across the ocean of delusion to the bright land of our true self!

THE DISTRESS OF STRESS

Within each of us there is a bounty of great wisdom that we connect with in those quiet times when we are alone with ourselves. However, the confusions and stresses we invariably have to deal with easily accumulate and crowd out those quiet times, so that we lose touch with our deeper purpose and direction.

By definition, disease implies that we were once at ease and then we lost that ease and became dis-eased. Traumatic experiences, hardships, fears of the future, worries and concerns – all these serve to throw us off balance, to overwhelm us with distress and to add to the inner tension and confusion. The mind clings to hurtful situations and plays them over and over in our search for answers. A thought becomes an idea, then an action, then a habit, then a neurosis or even a psychosis. A stressful thought arises in our minds and quickly becomes distressing. Pressures build and we lose control. Stress is the number one killer in the world today. In *Time* magazine we read:

> Two-thirds of office visits to family doctors are prompted by stress-related symptoms. Stress-related absenteeism, company medical expenses and lost productivity [in America] may cost between $50–75 billion [£30–50 billion] a year. Stress is now known to be a major contributor, either directly or indirectly, to six of the leading causes of death in the US, namely coronary heart disease, cancer, lung ailments, accidental injuries, cirrhosis of the liver, and suicide. The three best-selling prescription medications in the US (Valium, Inderal and Tagament) treat problems either caused or aggravated by stress, namely anxiety, hypertension and ulcers.

Stress is now an undeniable factor in most people's lives. It leads to reactionary and abusive behaviour, emotional breakdowns, psychological suffering and physical illness. What is known as 'the stress response' can be triggered by something as simple as a painful memory or someone shouting at us. An alarm sounds in the hypothalamus in the brain. The body is then alerted to start resisting the effect of the stress; when it can resist no longer, it becomes exhausted.

Physiological stress affects the nervous system, the muscles and the hormone balance; these are eased only nominally by such activities as watching television or going on holiday.

160

Emotional stress arises from desires being unfulfilled and from trying to live up to expectations. In the process we get caught between these opposites. The conflict is deeply rooted in our inability to express our feelings, so the stressed emotions become buried in the unconscious. Psychological stress arises due to repetitive mental thought patterns, confused and fearful mental activity, and endless internal chatter. There is little or no space in which to be quiet.

The stressed mind creates barriers that seem impossible to deal with and concerns itself in endless delusion. We are influenced by what other people think and feel; we react to simple issues as if they were matters of life and death; we are unsure what to do or how to make decisions; we easily become irrationally angry or upset. To release the stress we have to go deep enough for the buried impressions to begin to surface. We release these impressions by entering into the spaciousness that is beyond the content of the mind.

INNER CONSCIOUS RELAXATION

We usually think of relaxation as taking a break from routine: sitting in a comfortable chair and reading the paper, going to bed with a good book, putting our feet up and stretching out, going to a movie, having a cocktail, or lying on a beach, getting some sun and having nothing to do. But in our search for Shangri-la we rarely find what we bargained for! More often we are like the musk deer that has a beautiful smell in its belly, but spends its time searching the forest for this smell. We search for relaxation and ease by trying to find the perfect environment, the best movie, the ideal holiday.

Recently we went to Costa Rica. It sounded like the perfect place: hot sun, white, sandy beaches, warm water, palm trees. We wanted to go to some faraway place, get off the plane, and be close to a warm, quiet, empty beach! When the plane landed we had a four-hour bumpy bus ride to the beach, where lots of other people were all looking for the same thing. And it was pouring with rain. When we went for breakfast it was a battle between us and the

161

When we practise deep relaxation we go on a different journey. It is an exploration within ourselves to a place where the colours are bright and the sounds are sweet. A place where the tension is eased, where there is peace. We emerge refreshed, revitalized and renewed.

Conscious relaxation acts like the erase button on a tape recorder, so we can ease and remove repressed habits and attitudes, whether they are ill feelings from past abuse, or just little irritations. All of our conscious and unconscious experiences, thoughts, desires and conflicts are impressed in the grey matter of the brain. Like the bottom of a well that may have all sorts of things in it – an old shoe, a clock, a bucket or spoon – so in the depths of the mind there are many untold memories, long-forgotten images, hurt feelings, resentments, traumas and prejudices. Through systematically relaxing the mind we access the experiences impressed there and release any associated tension.

Like a cassette tape that has impressed on it a song, a drama or music, so our own dramas get played out in our minds, influencing how we feel, how we live, causing mood changes and fluctuations. Those things which we don't like get repressed and pushed down. They go deeper and then become more difficult to release. Relaxation is essential if we are to heal the deeper recesses of the mind, to learn to respond from a clear space rather than react from a past experience. For instance, Claire came to one of our workshops. She started the programme in a nervous and very fragile space:

I had begun to experience frequent and extreme mood swings. This gradually got worse until it felt like a dark cloud over my life. Everything I did seemed pointless: no enthusiasm, negative thinking, fear of going out and being with people, no heart to make conversation, feeling physically ill; I would ignore the

162

doorbell and telephone, shut myself away, always in tears and unable to relax. Realizing that I could not take much more of this constant fear, I was prescribed anti-depressants, but as soon as the pills ran out my symptoms returned. While waiting to see the doctor again I picked up a leaflet about a healing workshop. I knew I had to go. I had no idea what sort of weekend was ahead, but slowly, slowly I began to relax for the first time in so long. Towards the end, I could not hold back the tears. I felt so released from the burden of my traumatic past. It was replaced by an inner freedom and the strength to forgive. I feel I have come back to the land of the living.

CLAIRE EVANS

The practice described in detail at the end of this chapter – Inner Conscious Relaxation (ICR) – is a contemporary form of an ancient practice of relaxation that has been used throughout the ages to bring about a profound level of ease. It has a powerful healing effect. As a technique it is practical and easy to do because little effort is required; it can also be used whenever or wherever you want. It is a withdrawal of the mind from the senses, a bringing of the mind inwards to the source of peace, like a calm lake. There are no sense impressions, just an abundant creativity. It is not sleep, yet it is more relaxing. One hour of ICR is equal to four hours of deep sleep.

The human body is like a chemical factory – a laboratory of chemical processes, with hormones, enzymes, fluids, tissues and organs all working together. Physical, mental and emotional energies combine and interact in a way that enable our being to function. ICR systematically works to promote the chemical activity that stimulates optimum healing, well-being and peace of mind. Through releasing and relaxing, balancing and tuning the subtle systems, we create a more harmoniously functioning organism.

To enter into a deeply relaxed state it is essential that we make a commitment to set regular time aside. To take the time to be with ourselves, quietly, without distractions. Once a day is best, perhaps in the morning when we are not too sleepy, or early evening when we return from work, or late evening when it is quiet. It is good to choose a time and place when and where we will not be disturbed.

Fifteen minutes a day is better than an hour once a week, unless that is the only time available. Practising as often as possible will give most benefit, as this creates the space in which we can become familiar with relaxation, and, like any exercise, we will slowly become more proficient. It is also important to make sure we are warm enough, that we are wearing loose, comfortable clothing with no tight belts, watches, distracting jewellery or glasses. When we turn our awareness inwards we need to be as comfortable as possible. This form of relaxation is not a lazy, unconscious slumber; it is an alive and refreshing process.

At the beginning and end of the ICR practice there is a space to make an affirmation or resolve. In the East this is called a *sankalpa*. When we are in a deeply relaxed state and we make a resolve, that affirmation enters into the subconscious. We therefore make a resolve that will affect our whole life. We are planting a seed in the subconscious that will free the energy within us. It will then attract to us whatever is necessary to bring fruition. It is like bringing a flashlight into a dark tunnel: we begin to see our way more clearly.

Formulating our resolve gives us the opportunity to focus on our real purpose. Take some time to find a resolve that works for you. Having found it, stay with that resolve, at least for a while. Let it build momentum in your subconscious. Focus on whatever you feel is your life's purpose – that which you would most like to achieve in your life. Some examples are:

- I am healing and becoming whole.
- I am at peace within myself and at peace with all others.
- I am a vehicle of peace and healing.
- I am fearlessness in all situations.
- I am practising harmlessness to both myself and all others.
- May I be an instrument of self-realization for the benefit of all whom I meet.

164

During the practice of ICR we maintain a stream of un-broken awareness. We are simply the witness, aware and free of judgement. The thinking mind is not involved, so it does not resist or comment on what is taking place. We become de-tached from the process by just witnessing whatever arises and staying with the practice. Within this detached state, the prac-tice leads us through various stages and visualizations. Through these visualizations the impressions are released from the unconscious; the images created act as a catalyst, similar to the way that a dream can resolve conflicts and past experiences. However, rather than being forgetful and un-clear as we may be after a dream, here we are awake and alert. In this way we enter the unconscious with the conscious mind, releasing the contents – the habits, tensions and dramas – that prevent us from finding the freedom that is our natural state.

Deep relaxation takes us beyond the superficial pleasures and pains of life to a more peaceful and compassionate exis-tence. We think clearly, act spontaneously, have greater confi-dence, make more meaningful decisions. We see into things that were previously obscured. To be relaxed does not imply being dull; rather, it is a state of attentiveness, a dynamic process that produces feelings of invigoration, revitalization, calm and bliss. Tension and stress are removed and we see life in a new way. We see the sun shining rather than the clouds that obstruct.

Through relaxation and meditation we unfold the vast inner world that lies hidden at the core of our being. Just as there is a wealth of minerals and natural resources in the earth, so there is also a wealth buried inside us that is ready to be mined and discovered. Firstly through relaxation, and then meditation, we can dig deep. This gem-like quality is there waiting to be found.

THE HEART OF MEDITATION

True meditation is a fully conscious, natural awareness, a mind that is clear and free. Perhaps it has happened to you when you were walking along an empty beach, through a quiet wood, or perhaps lying in the bath or even doing the ironing! It can happen in a crowded street or in open moorland. It is the moment when 'I', as a separate entity, completely dissolves and merges with everything else. You become the rock you are sitting on and at the same time you are the water and the sound of the water and the bird swooping above and the clouds in the sky. You merge into all things, so there is no more 'I' being aware. There is just a complete oneness, an empty fullness, where all things are simply as they are.

Such a spontaneous experience can come and go at different times in our lives. The purpose of meditation practice is to free the mind of limitations so that we come closer to experiencing this state at all times. Meditation practice provides a structure for the mind to become focused and one-pointed, as opposed to being distracted or scattered. When the mind becomes inwardly focused we see the content more objectively, we can witness the thoughts, dramas, feelings, dreams and fears as they come and go, like birds in a clear sky. And we are able to see that beneath them is a quiet stillness. In the spaciousness that silence creates we meet ourselves, we have the chance to get to know ourselves: to listen, find out and explore, to internalize rather than externalize. This is a rare and wonderful opportunity.

Throughout the ages, meditation has been used to enter within and explore the wonders that are there. Whether we practise for just fifteen minutes a day or go into a long period of retreat does not matter. We are opening our doors of perception; we are removing the barriers that limit our healing. As J. Krishnamurti said, 'Meditation is not a means to an end. It is both the means and the end.'

Through relaxation we can enter into the deeper state of meditation. If we do not relax first, meditation can appear to be a struggle; we bring to our practice all the stress and tension in our lives and, as soon as we sit down to quieten the mind, the stress becomes highlighted. Within a few minutes our thoughts are working overtime, our bodies start aching and do not want to keep still, we long to be elsewhere, we feel inadequate and presume that meditation is beyond us. Yet it is not. It is simply that we are not relaxed enough to feel at ease in ourselves – our body is too full of tension and our mind is not familiar with being quiet. In *First Steps*, William Bloom says:

> This is basically the agony and the ecstasy of meditation. The ecstasy is the deep relaxation, calm and communion with the sacred. The agony is that it is difficult to start a meditation practice. . . . We experience acute discomfort, our minds begin a lunatic psychobabble and endless itches and fidgets torture us.

Knowing that these experiences can, and probably will, happen is some reassurance and gives us the strength to persevere. When we practise meditation we try to do it in a quiet place, and yet we may have an endless internal dialogue that is very noisy! As the external distractions dissolve, so the internal distractions take over. Such distractions can be boring, uplifting, nonsensical, foolish, chattering, jumbled or insightful; it all crowds in.

It is not uncommon to get over-involved with our thinking, as the chatter is endless. All sorts of thoughts appear in our day-to-day life, but we either pay them little attention or they seduce us into endless dramas. In meditation, paying attention is part of the practice. To see and to let go. It is when we hold on that the dramas take over.

> *I was explaining how, while we are meditating, anything can come into our minds, even thoughts like 'I want to kill my mother.' Although this is quite an intense thought, it happens. It does not mean that we really want to do it. Janet said, 'How did you know? I had that thought and then thought I must be a terrible person for thinking like that and I wanted to commit suicide!' Something that had started as a random thought had grown out of all proportion. Such thoughts arise. We have the choice to accept them or to release them. In another situation, Jackie told us her meditation was going very well until the thought of fish and chips arose in her mind! Then she could think of nothing else. Eventually she had to go and get some. It helps not to meditate at times when we are very hungry!*

EDDIE

167

Learning how to quieten the mind and relax the body so that meditation comes more easily simply takes time. That is why it is called practice. As we continue it begins to feel more natural, for ultimately it is our most ordinary state. In *No Destination*, Satish Kumar talks with a Franciscan friar:

> The friar said, 'Often people start to pray or meditate and they get impatient. The first lesson is to learn to be patient. You have to paint many paintings and only one or two of them will be the ones you feel satisfied with. You need to play music for hours to get to a moment of ecstasy. The Japanese spend twelve years in order to learn flower arrangement. A student spends seven years learning medicine. But when people seek to learn meditation or the art of praying, they want to do it in one day. The path of prayer is not for the impatient. Prayer is not just kneeling down in a chapel and saying the words; one's whole life is prayer.'

There are numerous forms of meditation practice – as many as there are personality types. There is no one way that is right for everyone. Each type of practice primarily has the same aim, that of providing a way for the mind to be absorbed. As the mind becomes focused, true meditation arises. The type or technique of meditation is, therefore, less important than is the intent of the practitioner.

Meditation practice is simply paying attention to whatever the object of the practice may be, and allowing that attentiveness to fill our whole being. The practice may involve watching our breath, the recitation of a mantra or sacred sound, the visualization of an image, or the flame of a candle being envisaged with our eyes open and then with our eyes closed. We focus on the object and simply witness thoughts and feelings as they arise, sounds as we hear them, distractions as just distractions, without giving them attention.

Watching and following the flow of the breath is a very simple and direct form of meditation practice which has been used throughout the ages. Paying attention to it creates a naturally inward focus. The rhythm of the breath is the rhythm of all life; by focusing on the breath and merging with it we merge into the experience of unity. On p. 174-5 there is a detailed description of a traditional breathing meditation.

We may find it easier to begin meditation with a group and a teacher rather than on our own; there are others with similar interests, and the group energy creates an atmosphere conducive to meditation. The teacher or guide keeps us on track and helps to show us the way. Alternatively, we can gather a few of our own friends to practise together.

When we are practising meditation, we need to do it without any ulterior purpose. Just to be in the here and now without any thought of the future, of a goal, or of achieving anything. If our purpose is to achieve a quiet mind and we start *trying* to do this, the trying itself creates a tension, becomes a distraction and defeats our goal. In the wanting of something to happen, there is a lack of space in which it can happen. It is important not to create any anxiety in the mind when we practise. The attitude with which we come to meditation should be one of simply being with the practice and watching whatever arises.

As with relaxation, it is helpful to practise meditation regularly and to find a suitable time of day when you will not be disturbed. Choosing a consistent place and time helps a great deal, as does creating a warm and loving environment – a familiar space we can enter into. There will always be things to pull us away from practising, especially at the beginning – it is quite normal to find endless excuses! However, it is at these times that even five minutes of just sitting quietly can help us in untold ways. Try it and see. Start with a few minutes each day and let it grow longer as you feel more comfortable. Like any new practice, it takes time to get used to and a commitment to maintain. The wandering mind is extremely habitual and does not want to become focused. Know how easily it can sway you!

Meditation practice is usually done in a seated position. This does not mean that you have to sit in a cross-legged posture on the floor, unless you feel comfortable. In the East, all sitting activities are done in this position because it is most natural for people from this part of the world; whereas in the West we have accustomed our bodies to sitting in chairs. If you want to develop a cross-legged posture, then try practising it at different times, not only when you are meditating. Sit that way to read a book or watch television. Experiment sitting with different-sized cushions so that your spine is supported in an upright position and your legs relaxed on the floor. If your feet fall asleep during the practice, just gently and mindfully stretch them out until the blood returns.

There is no need to try to maintain a posture that is causing pain. Meditation is something to be enjoyed. What is the purpose if it causes pain or further distraction? If you find it easier, use a straight-backed chair. What is important is that your spine is straight without being rigid, relaxed without being floppy. The idea is to remain alert and focused, without drifting off to sleep or getting caught up in endless dramas in the mind. When we become still in this way, we have the opportunity to connect with a great beauty within.

I read a short article on meditation and instinctively I knew how to do it without being taught. I would sit, breathe deeply and easily transport myself into a peaceful state. It was like coming home again or discovering a much-loved gift that I had put away in a drawer for later use and forgotten. During and after meditation I began to see and feel again the vibrant energies that I had experienced in early childhood.

DAVID LAWSON

Prayer too is a form of meditation, one in which the 'I' dissolves into the experience of love for the spiritual force in the universe. It need not be formal prayer but may be expressed in poetry, as a song, or as a mantra, chanting or bhajan, where we open our heart to dissolve into the heart of the divine. It is an expression of love, an offering to our higher self, the limited to the unlimited, where the drop merges with the ocean. It is an expression of our gratitude for the glory of life. Putting our heart into the words we speak is prayer. Father Edward Hays says, 'To pronounce your own unique word is to pray the most beautiful – if not the holiest – of prayers.'

PRACTICE

Inner Conscious Relaxation (ICR)

Take twenty to thirty minutes for this practice. Either record this practice on a tape, ask a friend to read it to you, or there is a tape available by the authors (see page 219). Find a quiet place either to lie on the ground or to sit in a chair. If you are lying on the ground have a blanket or mat beneath you, a pillow under your head, and a thin blanket to cover you. Your arms are parallel next to your body with your palms upward, your legs are slightly apart and your eyes are closed. If you are sitting, use a straight-backed chair, have your feet flat on the ground, with your hands resting on your thighs or in your lap, palms upward. Relax your body physically by finding a position you know you can keep throughout the practice.

Inner Conscious Relaxation is a practice of conscious awareness where your eyes are closed but you are not asleep and you are not externalized. That space within you, between sleep and the external, is where the practice takes place. It is important not to sleep. Stay with the practice no matter what may arise. It is not a practice of concentration or meditation; it is simply maintaining an unbroken stream of awareness. In this way you enter into the essence of your being.

If you become distracted, or your mind drifts at any time, come back to the practice. The point is to be able to move along through the practice as best you can; there is nothing for you to do except to stay with the instructions and not to sleep.

Now relax the body mentally. Do this by bringing your awareness to your toes and then work your way up through your body. Use your mind like a flashlight, releasing tension wherever it may appear: the toes, feet, ankles, calves, knees, thighs, buttocks, back of the body, front of the body, genitals, pelvis, stomach, navel, chest, fingers, hands, wrists,

171

elbows, upper arms, shoulders, neck and head.

Now become aware of your breathing. As you follow these instructions, stay with your breathing. Repeat silently to yourself, 'I am aware I am going to practise Inner Conscious Relaxation.' Repeat this three times. Watch the incoming and the outgoing breath, inhaling and exhaling naturally but with awareness.

Next you create a resolve – a statement or affirmation concerning your life. Resolves made in life may or may not come true, but the resolve made at the beginning and end of ICR will come true. A resolve is a simple sentence that concerns something you know you want to achieve or accomplish in this life. It is your heartfelt purpose. Try to create your resolve, either now or the next time you do the practice. Use the same resolve each time you do ICR. Now repeat your resolve three times silently to yourself. At the end of the practice, when you hear the words 'Peace . . . Peace . . . Peace', again repeat it three times to yourself.

You are now ready for the first stage of the practice: rotation of the mind through the various parts of the body. As each part of the body is mentioned, repeat it to yourself silently and try to visualize the part in your mind, moving through the body at a slow pace. For example, right hand thumb. Repeat 'Right hand thumb' and visualize the right hand thumb.

We begin: right hand thumb . . . second finger . . . third finger . . . fourth finger . . . fifth finger . . . (staying with the practice and not sleeping) palm . . . wrist . . . forearm . . . elbow . . . upper arm . . . shoulder . . . armpit . . . waist . . . hip . . . thigh . . . knee . . . calf . . . ankle . . . heel . . . sole . . . ball of the right foot . . . toes: the big one . . . second . . . third . . . fourth . . . fifth . . . left hand thumb . . . second finger . . . third . . . fourth . . . fifth . . . palm . . . wrist . . . forearm . . . elbow . . . upper arm . . . shoulder . . . armpit . . . waist . . . hip . . . thigh . . . knee . . . calf . . . ankle . . . heel . . . sole . . . ball

172

of the left foot . . . toes: the big one . . . second . . . third . . . fourth . . . fifth . . . right shoulder blade . . . left shoulder blade . . . spinal cord . . . left buttock . . . right buttock . . . both together . . . genitals . . . pelvis . . . stomach . . . navel . . . right chest . . . left chest . . . hollow of the chest . . . neck . . . chin . . . upper lip . . . lower lip . . . both lips together . . . nose . . . nose tip . . . right cheek . . . left cheek . . . right temple . . . left temple . . . right ear . . . left ear . . . right eye . . . left eye . . . right eyelid . . . left eyelid . . . right eyebrow . . . left eyebrow . . . centre of the eyebrows . . . forehead . . . top of the head . . . back of the head . . . whole body, whole body, whole body . . . awareness of the whole body. Repeat this, moving through the body again, but this time a little faster.

Now we work with the pairs of opposites. Create the feeling of heaviness in the physical body . . . feel your legs are heavy . . . your buttocks are heavy . . . your back is heavy . . . your arms are heavy . . . your chest is heavy . . . your head is heavy . . . your whole body is feeling heavy . . . feel as if your whole body is sinking into the ground and is getting heavier and heavier. Feel as if your body is so heavy you could not even lift your arms. Gather those images that are associated with heaviness and experience them in your body . . . stay with this for a few moments . . . visualize what it is to be heavy . . . a lead weight is heavy.

Now create the feeling of lightness in the physical body . . . what is lightness? A feather is light . . . bring the feeling of lightness to the body . . . to your fingers . . . your palms . . . your arms . . . stomach . . . chest . . . back . . . shoulders . . . neck . . . top of the head . . . whole body, your whole body is light . . . feel as if you are floating off the ground . . . stay with this for a few moments.

What is the feeling of coldness? Can you create the feeling of coldness in your body? Your hands are cold . . . your feet are cold . . . your buttocks are cold . . . your back is cold . . . you can feel a chill up your spine . . . your cheeks are cold . . . your head is cold . . . your whole body is getting colder and colder. . . . What is cold? It is a wintry day and you are walking in the snow, it is very cold outside . . . gather the images of coldness, create coldness in the whole body . . . pause for a few moments.

Now, what is heat? Can you create heat in your body? Gather those images associated with heat and create the feeling of heat . . . in the palm of your right hand . . . in your left hand . . . create heat in the sole of your right foot . . . your left foot . . . heat in your stomach . . . your chest . . . your lips . . . your eyes . . . your head . . . create heat in the whole of your body . . . it is a hot summer day and you are in the desert, the noonday sun is above . . . you feel the heat and are sweating . . . stay with this for a few moments.

Now you are ready for the next stage of ICR. Become aware of your heart. Feel as if you are entering your heart. Visualize in your heart that you are in a cave, and as you walk into the cave it seems to get bigger and bigger. As you keep walking, keep breathing into your heart. As you walk you see animals: a lion, tiger, cobra, elephant, deer and monkey. The animals are peaceful and friendly. You feel full of love and peace. Inside the cave there is a fire with a holy woman, a goddess, sitting in Nirvana – in ecstasy. When she sees you, she greets you and offers you a seat, and then you sit around the fire together. There is warmth, you feel at home, it is special. The sound of OM can be heard. The smell of incense is everywhere. The atmosphere is forgiving and fearless. In that moment you understand and realize the healing power of love. You feel her healing rays and thank the goddess, bowing your head in gratitude . . . stay with this for a while.

Now in this final stage of ICR we create visualizations by becoming aware of the space in the region of your fore-head, known as chidakash. As a visualization is created, try to visualize it in this open space as best as possible. If it is easy, fine; if not, just keep moving with the practice. Only do what you can.

174

Begin with a red rose * a child riding a bicycle on the road * a plane flying overhead * clouds in the sky * grey clouds * blue clouds * your physical body * you outside your physical body looking down at your body * a camel with two humps * a newborn baby * the Virgin Mary * a yogi sitting in meditation * a candle burning * the ocean * waves breaking on the shore * a person rowing on a lake * the ripples from the oars * a church * inside the church a preacher is giving a sermon * a golden cross * a dog barking * your physical body lying on the ground naked with a golden thread going upward from your navel * the Buddha * a palm tree * an oak tree * a large balloon high up in the sky * a mouse * a nun * a Christmas tree * a dead body * a policeman * the waves of the ocean * people sunbathing on the beach * a church choir * snow-capped mountains * a river rushing after a rainstorm * a garden where you are walking surrounded by all sorts of flowers: red ones, pink ones, yellow, purple, green, orange, blue and white ones * now visualize a tiny white light the size of a pin-point. Stay with the light and let it grow.

Peace, peace, peace. Become aware of the resolve that you made at the beginning of the practice of ICR . . . repeat it three times silently to yourself.

Now become aware of your breathing, watch the inhalation and exhalation . . . continue for a few moments. Become aware of the room you are in. Now move your fingers, then your toes . . . externalize your consciousness . . . keeping the eyes closed . . . the practice of ICR is over. When you are ready, slowly roll over on to your side. Stay there for a while. Then sit up with your eyes still closed. Have a smile on your face and greet the world as you open your eyes. Thank you.

Breath Awareness Meditation

This meditation practice focuses on the flow of the breath as it enters and leaves the body. Allow fifteen to thirty minutes for this practice. Either record this practice on a tape, ask a friend to read it to you, or there is a tape available by the authors.

Start by finding a comfortable seated position, whether sitting cross-legged on the floor with a straight back, or in an upright chair with your feet flat on the floor. The hands are resting in the lap or on the thighs. The eyes are closed. The head is relaxed, tilter neither up nor down. The spine is straight. Take a deep breath and feel at ease in your posture.

With this practice your breath is completely natural: it is neither forced nor hurried, neither slow nor heavy. Focus your attention on the flow of your natural breath, watching it come into your body and leave again. As the mind begins to quieten, so your attention becomes more focused on this rhythm of the breath.

Now bring your awareness to the belly area, which is rising and falling as the breath enters and leaves the body. Come to an area approximately two inches below the navel. This is known as the hara, an area of tremendous energy that is deep within your being.

Now start counting your breath. Do this by counting at the end of each out breath. Breathe in, breathe out, count 1. Breathe in, breathe out, count 2. Breathe in, breathe out, count 3. Continue in this way until you reach 10 and then start at 1 again, counting one number at the end of each out breath. If you lose the counting, or find you are counting beyond 10, then just bring your attention back and start at 1 again.

Your concentration is in the region of your hara, beneath the navel, and from there you are watching the rise and fall, in and out flow of the breath, counting at the end of each out breath. By focusing on the breathing and the counting, the mind becomes quiet and relaxed.

If thoughts arise, simply observe and label them 'thinking'. Let the thoughts go, like clouds in the sky. If any feelings arise, simply observe and label them 'feelings'. Let them go. Always come back to watching and counting the breath.

Make sure your spine is straight and upright and your body is at ease in its position. If the body is tense it will become distracting. Let it be at ease so your meditation can go deeper.

After five or ten minutes, instead of counting at the end of each out breath, start counting at the beginning of each in breath. So your practice goes like this: Count 1, breathe in, breathe out. Count 2, breathe in, breathe out. Count 3, breathe in, breathe out. And so on up to 10 and then back to 1 again. This shifts the focus of your concentration. Instead of becoming aware of the breath after you have breathed, you become aware of the breath before it enters your body.

Feel the rhythm of your breath as it enters and leaves – this is the universal rhythm of the tides, the winds and seasons. Your sense of the world around you withdraws into the silence of your own being. Your mind is becoming quieter, more focused upon this universal rhythm of which you are an integral part.

After a further five or ten minutes you can stop counting and simply be at one with the flow of the breath. In dropping the counting, you are also letting go of your separate, individual self and becoming one with the universal self. Simply focus on the breath as it enters and leaves your body.

Through the breath you merge with the universal self that contains all silence and all sound. As you become one with the rhythm of the breath, so you expand beyond your limitations, beyond the form and the boundaries that you impose. Through keeping your awareness in your hara

177

you are in touch with the earth, which is a part of this great rhythm. Your individual self dissolves into the earth, dissolves into the sky, and dissolves into the universal self.

There arises a great joy, a great opening of the heart, a softness, gentleness and compassion that radiate. As you breathe in, this softness and gentleness fill your whole being. As you breathe out you offer them to the world, to the universe. Breathing in compassion, breathing out joy and love. This joy is not yours to own, for it is universal in nature: it is the joy of life itself. Let the breath be a vehicle to send this joy and love outwards, ever outwards.

Now gently come back into yourself, becoming aware of the seat beneath you, the room you are in, and the world outside your room. Slowly open your eyes, and may the joy be with you wherever you go.

9

WALKING
THE
PATH

One turns in all directions and sees nothing.
Yet one senses that there is a source for this deep restlessness,
and a path that leads there is not a path
to a strange place, but a path home.

PETER MATTHIESSEN

As we proceed on our journey to wholeness, we soon realize we are travelling on a path. It is not an obvious path that clearly stretches ahead of us, but is one that is unfolding in each moment. Nor is it a straight path, but it twists and turns, goes up and down, is inevitably unpredictable, at times fearful and other times full of wonder. Occasionally we may think we have lost our way, such as when we slip into old patterns of reactive or habitual behaviour; or we get distracted and wander off, doing things that seem entirely contrary to healing. We then have to listen carefully to our inner voice in order to find our way again. Sometimes we feel as if we are backtracking, but although the landscape is familiar it is never quite the same as it was when we were first there. We may even think that nothing is happening, that it is just life in the same old way. Yet life itself, the path we are all on, is a journey.

The difference is that, as we become conscious of the path, we start to choose the direction in which we want to go, and we begin to make a committed effort to discover all that is involved in the journey. When we initially become aware that there is a path, we may feel a little uncertain about what to do or where it is leading us. Can we trust it? Are there any guidelines? Things can feel so new and unfamiliar that each step appears momentous!

Soon we learn to take just one step at a time, and to trust our feelings, however irrational they may be. As we proceed we become more confident, we get to know how the path looks in various guises, we get an indelible sense of where we are going and we begin to have more confidence in the process. The path becomes like a river flowing into the sea, moving with determination. In Buddhism this is called *Bodhicitta* – awakening, our will for enlightenment, the volition to find our way home, an inspiration beyond all desires.

We see the path most clearly when we look back at where we have come from. At all the varied events and situations in our lives – whether painful, difficult, frightening, wonderful or joyful – that have contributed to our growth and understanding. How each event led to the next that eventually brought us to this moment. Chance meetings, coincidences, decisions taken, things we may not have understood at the time – all have added to and shaped the person we are now. We have survived all sorts of crises, many different moments of uncertainty and trauma. We have even done things that we did not expect to do. What we have learnt forms the foundation from which we are now building.

Each one of us has our own path, born out of our life situations, but we inevitably share with others the maps, landmarks, scenery and signposts. And although each path is unique in its manifestation there is a central meeting place, for all are leading to a fuller, more enriching and uplifting life.

The journey may be a slow, step-by-step process through which we gradually deepen our understanding and awareness. Or it may be that by confronting a personal crisis, perhaps

180

even the possibility of our own death, or during the 'dark night of the soul' when we are exposed to our deepest fears, our lives are irrevocably changed. A turning point is reached, sometimes lasting a few minutes, or perhaps spread out over some days or weeks, which moves us into a different state of being. In *Zen Flesh, Zen Bones*, Paul Reps says: 'It can happen to you. In a flashing moment something opens. You see the same unsame world with fresh eyes. It doesn't make sense. It makes you.'

Having sunk into the depths of pain and suffering, of immanent loss, this is the moment when we start to climb upwards; trapped in confusion and chaos, it is when clarity and understanding begin to beckon. We awaken to the possibility of our healing. The following stories are examples of such a turning point.

I had come to realize that I was wasting my life chasing after people and emotional experiences that were not making me happy. In so doing I had extinguished a sense of spiritual life that I had once known vividly. As a child I had felt the world around me was full of wonder and mystery; but as I grew older I had rejected those feelings and all the attractions of the social world had taken over. Now I was feeling deeply remorseful and depressed, believing that I had lost for good something that was infinitely precious. One night I could not sleep. I was engulfed by sadness and repentance. All night I paced up and down, longing to reconnect with this sense of the sacred. When the morning light came I looked into the garden and saw a blackbird. Suddenly it was as if I had never seen a blackbird before! I felt that this blackbird was the most real thing I had ever seen. Just seeing it in this new way was enough to make life worth living.

In the following days I became intensely aware of sound and light, and one evening, as I looked at a rhododendron flower, I began to feel a sense of communication with it, as though it and I had become one. It came to me that the whole mystery of existence was not so far away but actually very close at hand, and that the secret lay in my relationship with everything around me. The sense of oneness I had just felt with a flower seemed to have happened because I was still, not wanting anything, and therefore free to see it properly and to know it as itself. A few days later I put on some

181

music. As the first note of the music sounded there was an almost audible click in my mind and I found everything transformed. I was in a different state of consciousness. It was as though the separate feeling of 'me' had gone and instead there was a great sense of clarity, of utter beneficent wonderful emptiness. And in that emptiness there were no barriers.

ANNE BANCROFT

I was flying from New York to Dallas. It was a late-night flight, quite a small plane with only a few passengers, so we all had a row of seats to ourselves and most of us were sleeping. Somewhere near Dallas the plane caught the tail end of a tornado. As we were jerked out of our sleepiness the plane became like a feather in the sky. It seemed impossible that we could survive. I began preparing myself to die and it felt OK. But then the thought suddenly arose that if I died I would not be able to tell the people whom I loved that I loved them. Suddenly love began pouring through me, filling my entire being with a power and magnificence I had not known before. Nothing else existed but this love, supporting, holding, caressing. At about the same time the plane began to pull out of the tornado and eventually landed some 200 miles away. The experience stayed with me. In the weeks that followed I found myself in an altered state of awareness, living in an experience of love that seemed to emanate from the very essence of life itself. It was like becoming a child again, a rapture and freedom bubbling up from within, a joyful ecstasy!

DEBBIE

It was not until my mid-twenties that I began to realize that my lingering discontent with life was not because of outer circumstances but on account of my inner world. It was somehow arid. My outer world was full of people and events but they were all substitutes, in some way, for an inner depth I could not seem to grasp. I felt cut off from being able to really experience joy and beauty, from being able to allow love and affection to come to me. Looking back at this period it was as if I existed in life but I never knew how to live properly. Then, while on a trip to Mexico, I stumbled across an ancient sacred temple, hidden in the middle of the jungle. It was completely covered in creepers. I remember

*thinking, 'That's like me! My whole psyche is entwined with vines
and creepers. What is ancient and genuine about me is quite
hidden. All I see, and all others probably see when they look at me,
are the creepers which obscure.' I felt disturbed and ashamed. As if
a tiny window in me had opened, just a fraction. But enough to
make me determined to do something about it.*

SERGE BEDDINGTON-BEHRENS

*One day in September, I was skiing on St Mary's Glacier in
Colorado. I carried my skis and poles, wore my ski boots, and
walked 1,400 feet up into the glacier. After skiing on the top of the
glacier for a while, I then skied over to the far side. It was my first
serious year of skiing. Suddenly I got too close to the side, fell
backwards and began tumbling hundreds of feet down the face of
the glacier. Because I fell backwards I had absolutely no control. I
felt that this was it, my life was finally over, it seemed inevitable.
Yet as I kept falling I felt euphoric and clear! I was a spectator
and it was like I was watching a movie, except I was the movie. I
couldn't believe I felt so happy and yet my life was about to be over!
I kept falling until, at the bottom, I suddenly saw rocks ahead.
Surely this was going to be my final moment? Yet miraculously I
rolled on to a flat slab of rock. I lay there, the broken toe piece from
my skis next to me, surprised that I was still alive. I felt I was in a
state of grace. And I knew there was something, some force, that
was holding this life together and that for some reason my time was
not yet up. I was determined to discover that reason.*

EDDIE

*In my mid-forties my life quite suddenly and unexpectedly began
to fall apart. Predictability and control gave way to tremendous
confusion. Issues of communication, relationships and identity
reached crisis proportions as my marriage faltered, friendships
faded and I spent my time alone and depressed. During this time I
had a recurring dream from which I would awake in a cold sweat.
In the dream I am walking through a forest and come upon a
group of men dressed in black, standing around a grave. On the
ground lies a woman. The men wrap her naked body in a blanket
and proceed to lower it into the grave. They are expressionless and
silent. As they cover her with earth I become very alarmed as I*

183

know that she isn't dead! As the men walk away I rush to the grave and begin digging with my hands until I feel her body. I uncover her body. She gasps. I wake up.

Some time later I told a friend about this dream and that it felt incomplete. She offered to help me complete it while in a waking state. I agreed to try. I focused on the point of awakening from the dream and continued: After a long struggle, I pull her out of the grave and down to a nearby stream. As I wash the soil from her face, her breathing becomes more regular and I feel a deep sense of relief. She begins to look familiar. She sits up, her face directly in front of me. She is a woman with my Slavic features. In fact, she is a female version of me! At this point the two identities become completely united. I was both the rescuer and the rescued, both he and she. The dream was over. This was a turning point in my life. I began to rediscover and nurture my own feminine nature. Sensitivity and compassion soon balanced the rational. With renewed determination I began to build bridges between my wife and myself, and to rekindle friendships. I began to feel like a complete human being for the first time in my life.

MIROSLAV BORYSENKO

The doctor diagnosed Hepatitis B and gave strict advice that I was to have complete rest. Unfortunately I worsened and became isolated in the Tropical Diseases ward. Five weeks later I was dying. As I slipped into a coma I remember looking down on myself from the ceiling. Then I was travelling along an upwardly steep tunnel and out into brilliant light, surrounded by the most beautiful scenery. A man was walking towards me. I kept asking him, 'Where am I? Where am I?' Before he could answer a group of people arrived, among them my parents. My mother was hugging me and dad was ruffling my hair – the loving feelings were overwhelming. It all seemed so natural, but how could this be happening? Everyone here was deceased. Was I dead? As I was thinking this question, my mother began to answer me, 'You must learn to breathe into your lungs again. Feel your hands becoming warm and move slowly back down into your body.' I didn't want to leave. But all I could hear was, 'Breathe deeply. Look at yourself, see your children.' My children's faces appeared and then, as if I was being pushed, I began to float back down the tunnel. 'Breathe

*deeply' were the words I was whispering as I came out of the coma.
I had been taught that breathing was a very precious gift. Over the
following weeks I started to recover and to fully live in this life.*

*At fourteen I felt less and less able to cope and I became
psychosomatically ill. I had frequent colds, headaches, stomach
cramps and vomiting fits that got steadily worse. At fifteen, two-
thirds of the way through my fourth year, I felt so lethargic that I
could barely drag myself out of bed. My body seemed almost too
heavy to move. I became more and more absent from school until
one morning I woke up knowing that I would never go to school
again. I never did. This whole period was like travelling through
a dark tunnel; a dark night of the soul. It was as if all the energy
that I had put into fitting into the world, keeping my heart closed,
keeping myself safe, dealing with the daily bombardment of other
people's feelings and negativity, all of it collapsed in on itself. So
many of my self-imposed limitations were dying and something
new was emerging. My heart, mind and spirit were beginning to
reopen and I was remembering my true nature.*

DAVID LAWSON

STEP BY STEP WE MAKE OUR WAY

From the above stories we see how the intensity of personal
experience can change our lives. A turning point is a powerful
motivator. But let it not appear that experiencing a turning
point is the only way to discover our healing. Such experiences
do not necessarily happen, or have to happen, to us all. The
gradual approach is far more likely, and certainly more enduring. Experiencing the dark night of the soul may lead us to
glimpsing the light, but without perseverance, commitment
and endurance we can soon slip into forgetfulness and lose our
way, returning to how we were before. The experience casts a
light on the path, but it is not the path itself. Although we have
had a profound realization, we now need to absorb this into
our whole being until it is fully embodied in our day-to-day
life.

185

True change takes time. We cannot become the perfectly healed, unconditionally loving, selfless, generous and complete human being we would like to be overnight! If we try too hard, it can lead to a dispirited sense of failure and hopelessness and we may even give up. We need the patience to go one step at a time. To be gentle and accepting of our failings and to honour our successes, to know that it is all right if we make a mistake and that no one will punish us. We may have many different experiences that are embarrassing when we look back, but it is from these experiences that we learn. They form the ground from which we grow.

In 1977, as a fairly successful and well-off professional architect and regular guy, eating tons of meat and a Mars bar a day, but with a vague feeling of 'There must be more to life than this', I took myself off on a trip to India and the East – quite unaware of the 'Exposure-to-India-can-totally-Alter-Your-Life' syndrome. I returned a bearded, vegetarian, hippie would-be writer. I proceeded to write a ten thousand-word novel in six weeks. But it wasn't until I encountered macrobiotics, the following year, that any consciously spiritual factor emerged. Somehow, I intuitively knew that this weird brown-rice culture could lead me towards understanding what my life was for. I had to wade through some years of obsession with food and organ sickness, but I did get a bit healthier, learn meditation and realize that difficulties are not the end of the world but are, indeed, some of our main vehicles for growth. For the first time I gained a basic sense of appreciation for being alive. My perception is that many of us work away on our path and for years it may seem that we're not getting anywhere. But eventually moments of breakthrough do come, like green shoots in the spring.

GERRY THOMPSON

In describing the journey, another image we can use is that of the mud, the stem and the lotus flower. The mud represents our issues, the experiences, traumas, conflicts, pain and confusion – all the difficulties we are working with and have to confront on our journey to wholeness. The stem is the work we do with all of this, the continual perseverance even if we feel we

186

cannot go on and all our efforts appear meaningless. This is the willingness to be honest and not to hide behind falsehoods; it is the compassion we apply, accepting and embracing whatever arises; it is our commitment to our own sanity and peace. The lotus grows out of the mud, yet it emerges free of the mud, stainless and beautiful. The flower is our healing, the realization of who we really are, the emergence of the luminous, loving self; it opens naturally as a result of our effort.

The beauty of this image is that of seeing the essential nature of the mud. Without it there can be no flower. In other words, it is through our pain and suffering that we can find a deeper joy; it is not by denying the pain, for denial will create even greater pain. The stem emerges as we slowly wade through the mud, become familiar with it, apply effort, and learn how to use it as nourishment for the flower.

This image – that of the mud, stem and flower – is a way of illustrating how our issues are not so unique. Mud is something we each have to deal with, and no particular mud is worse than anyone else's! It is normal to feel that our own issues are special, that no one else can understand, that everyone else's life is working except ours. Why do others have it together and not me? But we only have to compare notes to find that mud is universal, that the experience of being immersed in mud is shared by all. It is our commitment to moving through and beyond the mud that enables the flower to open.

At the age of seven my mam threw my dad out of the house. I felt my heart close. I hated the fact that he lived in a men's hostel and all my years growing up this was my mam's fault. It tore me apart. I don't recollect any kisses and cuddles and well into adult life I felt unloved, unwanted and uncared for. When dad left we were living in what was to become the slum clearance area. My brother and I used to sell papers on Saturday evenings. I also used to wheel the pram with washing into the wash-house so mam could catch the bus. I could have died from shame. At twenty years old I married the first man who had ever cared about me and we had two children. My life went downhill from then on.

I believe I was suffering from post-natal depression. I worked evenings in the local pub and drank more than I sold. I was seeing the doctor for 'nerves' and he prescribed an opium-based tonic which I was soon addicted to. My life was like a haze. I became addicted to anti-depressants and tranquillizers. I had a locked drawer full of pills and would panic if there was a chance of running short of anything. Finally I swallowed a load of pills and took myself off to a quiet area to die. But I didn't think the pills were working, so I went to the pub for a drink. To me, God then intervened, disguised as an ambulance driver who was in the pub. He recognized the symptoms and had me whisked off to hospital for a stomach pump. I hated him for saving me. I now had extra problems: self-hatred, shame, failure, remorse. My life seemed to be going in circles. The same horrible feelings, the despair, the helplessness. I tried suicide and failed yet again.

I had to do something. I decided to kick the 'tonic' so I changed doctors and found one who would no longer supply me. This was the first step in a long, slow emergence. I was referred to a psychiatric counsellor. Anything was better than walking around as a doped-up zombie receiving electro-cardiac therapy in a psychiatric ward. I had counselling therapy for ten years and also medically supervised LSD therapy. Towards the end of the seventies I got a book from the library – Richard Hittleman's 28-day yoga plan. I started to work on it religiously and then joined a yoga class. That was it! It really was like seeing the light! I was at group therapy one day when I realized that I no longer needed to be there. My psychiatrist had been a wonderful crutch but I no longer needed one. I had become a different person. Without even noticing it I was off the tranquillizers and anti-depressants, and in 1980 I stopped drinking.

I realized that we should do unto others as we would have them do unto us. I realized that what we fear we bring about. I suffered for my stealing. I suffered for my infidelity. I suffered for all my wrong actions. I realized the law of cause and effect. I have met some special people, sometimes just crossing paths for a very short time, who turned my world around, who opened my heart, who made me trust, who stopped me holding a bit of myself in reserve, who gave me a feeling of 'all-one-ness' instead of 'aloneness'. Yoga allowed my heart to open and enabled me to love myself, and then to share this love with everyone. It is crystal-clear to me that the thirteen years of hell that I went through was to teach me

something – it was a learning experience. Thank God I came out
of it a little nearer heaven then hell!

EILEEN CAUDWELL

SIGNPOSTS ALONG THE WAY

Given the effort that is needed to journey inwards, and the
unpredictable nature of the path itself, we could well be
forgiven for wondering if we were wise to start this journey at
all! We want to love unconditionally, but find that it means
having to deal with fear, bitterness and resentment; we want to
open our heart to ourselves and others, but find that we have to
confront everything that is keeping it closed. And there are few
clear signposts. We do not get told ahead of time what is going
to happen next, what we will be doing or which direction we
will be taking.

There are moments when it may appear that disintegration
is happening, when the familiar begins to crumble and
change. Nothing seems to be staying the same – earthquake
tremors are rumbling through our lives. It may be chaotic and
hard to comprehend. But if we trust in the process, we will
sense that integration is actually taking place. A breaking down
has to occur first: the old way has to go before the new comes. It
is important to remember that nothing is permanent, most
especially our state of mind! Everything is in constant change,
nothing stays the same for more than a moment, so we have to
be patient and to wait for the way through to appear.

And then life presented me with a challenge. I contracted a very
serious life-threatening disease and physically fell apart. And I
also fell crazily in love for the first time. So the rather rusty steel
gates protecting my somewhat unexercised and previously
wounded heart now clanged rather clumsily open! The love affair
did not work out, and the pain of that combined with the pain of
the illness served to break me down and somehow break up
something granite-like inside me. This enabled me to dissolve into
a deeper part of myself, to move beyond some of those tough outer
layers protecting my heart. I became quite naked and the heart that

189

I began to slowly discover was a tender and vulnerable one. It was soft and mushy, as inexperienced as it was wounded. But, to my horror, I also saw that it was full of rage and violence. In beginning to open to something new within me, I had to look at my own darkness and immaturity. I realized that if my life was to become remotely real, I had to do a great deal of inner work on myself.

SERGE BEDDINGTON-BEHRENS

One of the signposts that helps us to keep going in the right direction is the statement: 'Let go, let God.' This has an immediately releasing effect – it lets free the need to control, to be in charge, to hold on rigidly to plans and to fix how things will work or what will happen next. Instead, there is a surrendering of control and a willingness to let God – that higher force, the cosmic consciousness – into our lives.

This is not the same as shrugging off responsibility for our actions; neither does it mean sitting back and waiting for God or someone else to step in and take over. In no way does it mean a giving up of effort. To truly 'Let go, let God' is actually quite hard work! It is a partnership, a two-way relationship. To surrender is to release the needs of the ego and to trust in the process, and this in itself takes effort. It is also the faith in our own divinity. This is not a blind faith, as there is an awareness, an inner knowing that makes absolute sense. It is a gentle and soft surrendering, a sense of coming home, of going from the meaningless to the meaningful. To 'Let go, let God' is saying that we don't have to carry the whole world on our shoulders, it is recognising that we are a part of a greater reality. As the musician George Harrison said, it is 'within you and without you.'

Other important signposts or guides are practices such as Inner Conscious Relaxation, meditation, yoga, Tai Chi, Chi Kung and Akido, to mention only a few of the many available. These are valuable and sane methods that give us understanding and clarity on the path. Such practices keep us grounded, at ease and in touch with our inner selves. Most are ancient systems that have been used for hundreds of years. We can practise on our own, but it can be of tremendous value to participate in a meditation group, a yoga class or some similar type of gathering where we are able to meet others who are also journeying.

Enormous strength and support can be gained through sharing 'the agony and the ecstasy' of the path; the trials and tribulations are eased when experienced with fellow travellers. We so easily deny ourselves the chance to share our heart by locking the pain away and pretending that everything is going fine. This does not benefit us. Opening and sharing our inner world is essential for our healing; it gives us the chance to get in touch with our real feelings. In sharing, we know we are not alone. It also gives the person listening to us the chance to open themselves to giving and loving. To be a friend is to be aware and sensitive to another, to be there as a support when needed. True friends are fearless in showing their feelings and the extent of their caring.

In my early twenties, some male friends and I used to be stoned on hash almost every weekend for a year. At the end of that year my brain began to feel physically scrambled, I started having bad trips and knew that we were wasting our human potential. My best friend and I, after some trauma, decided to quit, which we did. Then I learned that a girl, who I was wildly attracted to, had some grass and was planning to get stoned on her own. Because I cared for her, I stormed into her room and started raging that what she was doing was self-destructive, harmful, etc. She stared at me, bewildered, then told me that what she did was entirely her own business and I had no right to interfere. I felt devastated. Tears welled to my eyes. I reached for the door, only to find her hand tugging on my arm. She said she had almost never seen a man cry before, and had never experienced such passionate concern for herself from another human being.

ARON GERSH

I was nineteen, at medical school, caught in a nightmare purgatory I didn't want to be in. I didn't want to be a doctor; I just wanted to be a healer. With sinking heart and sickening belly I had done the round of meeting the other students and going to physiology lectures. I didn't want to spend my youth here, learning

191

not to think, not to feel, not to question. But I still felt I had no choice, that I had to be there. A moment came, in a friend's kitchen, when I was going on and on about it all. John said, 'It sounds like you are saying you don't want to do medicine.' Clonk. The wheels hit the spinner. The spiral of chaos, of grief, fell down inside me, hit the ground and I stopped. My skies cleared. My pattern shifted. 'You're right, I don't.' That one simple intervention, for which I am forever grateful, changed my life.

SUSANNAH DARLING KHAN

As helpful and supportive as our friends are, there may also be times in our journey when we need to hear a less personally involved voice and we could benefit from counselling or therapy. The obstacles can seem insurmountable, the problems too difficult to solve on our own. We need an impartial opinion. Since the way forward is not always clear, we need support systems. Those who have gone ahead of us can offer valuable guidance. Finding someone we trust and feel comfortable with, who is warm and understanding, encourages us to open to ourselves. In sharing our innermost thoughts and feelings we are able to see more clearly. A good therapist enables us to connect with that which is holding us back and then lets us go ahead on our own. In *Bioenergetics*, Alexander Lowen describes:

In my view, therapy involves a voyage of self-discovery. It is not a short and simple journey, nor is it free from pain and hardship. There are dangers and risks, but then, life itself is not free from hazards, for it too is a journey into the unknown of the future. Therapy takes us backward into a forgotten past, but this was not a safe and secure time, else we would not have emerged from it scarred by battle wounds and armored in self-defense. It is not a journey I would recommend to make alone, although I am sure some brave people have made the trip unaided. A therapist acts as a guide or navigator. He has been trained to recognise the dangers and he knows how to cope with them; he is also a friend who will offer support and courage when the going gets rough.

192

THE GURU WITHIN

There may also be times when we find ourselves being drawn to a particular teacher, guru or religion. This attraction could last just a short time and simply be a part of our journey, or it may become our chosen path, exclusive of all other approaches. Such an attraction is an expression of the longing for the divine and for the sacred to be a part of our lives; we may feel closer to divinity when in the presence of a wise and helpful teacher than when we are on our own.

A teacher/student relationship can be of tremendous benefit. It provides us with a clear path to follow and support when issues arise. It also mirrors back to us the areas where healing is most needed. In this way, enormous insight can be gained into the many complexities of the human condition and the teachings that can guide us to our healing.

However, there are a few inherent drawbacks when we become close to a teacher or guru. For instance, there is the danger of believing that the teacher is a perfect being, incapable of making mistakes. That the teacher is beyond the normal human condition and is invincible, if not even God incarnate. As the teacher is responsible for our salvation, so he/she must be greater than any ordinary human. Having created such an image, it is then impossible to accept the very real humanness of the teacher. So if the teacher does something that displays the fact that he/she is, after all, just a human being, then we are bereft, helpless, lost.

And at that point, sadly, many people give up the journey. The teacher is equated with the teaching, so if the teacher fails the teaching itself must be at fault. There is a great disillusionment with the journey and all the learning and understanding already experienced are dismissed.

Such a situation occurs because there is also the tendency to lose touch with our own innate wisdom and to adopt whatever the teacher says as being the truth. Surely the teacher must know more than us, or they could not be a teacher, and therefore in comparison we must know very little. Having greater wisdom is what keeps the teacher ahead of us; believing we have very little wisdom keeps us in need of the teacher.

Many teachers thrive on having students and do not encourage them to find their own truth – rather, the students must hold to the truth as expressed by the teacher. When this happens it is very hard to leave the teacher and find our own path. We are locked into a dependent relationship; as we have no trust in our own understanding, we need the teacher as a guide.

Good teachers will not encourage such dependency but will empower their students to find and listen to their own wisdom. A genuine teacher is a compassionate friend, selfless, kind and generous. The great Indian holy man Ramana Maharishi explained how the guru is there to push you into yourself from the outside and to pull you into yourself from the inside, to reveal the guru or teacher within you. The Buddha said that no one should follow what he taught until we had first tried and tested it to be true for ourselves. In *The Way Ahead*, Yoko Ono says, 'Bless you for your search of direction for it is a sign of aspiration. Transform the energy to receptivity and the direction will come to you.'

It is, therefore, very important to remember that insight, wisdom and healing come from within us, that the teachers and the teachings are there simply as stepping stones, as a guide to help us along the path. They are not the path itself. To heal ourselves we have to acknowledge that the real guru is within – to thine own self be true! We learn to listen to the inner voice, to what the Quakers call 'the still small voice within'. To develop trust in ourselves and our own understanding. We are reminded of the Dalai Lama saying that we are all equal. Although others can guide, it is vital that we respect our intuition, our gut feeling, our own wisdom. Then we can take from the teachings what we need to assist our healing. As the philosopher Ralph Waldo Emerson said, 'Let us be silent, that we may hear the whisperings of the Gods.'

In the mid-1960s I began my search for truth with a keen sincerity. Before that, like my other friends, I went to the latest disco searching for whatever thrill and pleasure there was available. I was looking to be entertained by life. But then I began to feel a hunger inside that was different and needed my attention. I

194

was being drawn inward rather than outward. At that time a friend took me to a spiritual discourse with Swami Satchidananda, who had just arrived from Sri Lanka. He was tall with a long beard, and wore saffron robes. He was peaceful, radiant, friendly and wise. His very nature and gestures told me he had something to teach me. As I began to get more involved with Swami Satchidananda, I also met another teacher, Prabhupada. He was the founder of the Krishna Consciousness movement. In a little store front on Second Avenue, on the Lower East Side, was the beginning of one of the world's largest spiritual movements.

I was drawn to Prabhupada, also known as Swami Bhaktevedanta, by the sheer simplicity of his message. All that was needed was to chant the name of Krishna, as Krishna is said to remove the veil of Maya or ignorance. You become Krishna Conscious and return to Godhead, our true home. I felt great joy being with these sincere devotees, especially Prabhupada. We would take walks together each day at 6 a.m. But a difficulty arose for me when, on one occasion, he said that Krishna was the only way.

Soon after that I was at a large gathering at the Unitarian church on Central Park West to hear Swami Satchidananda give a talk. He asked if anyone had a question. I reluctantly raised my hand, fearful of making a fool of myself. I was very new at it all and found it difficult to speak in public. But I told him how Swami Bhaktevedanta had said that Krishna was the only way. Swami Satchidananda replied, 'I will not answer that question!' I felt myself sinking into my seat, fearing all eyes were on me. He then reversed his position and began to speak directly about it, saying, 'How can there be just one way?' He said this with so much compassion and love in his heart that it hit me like a bolt of lightning. He continued, 'There are as many ways as there are people. Each one of us is the way.' This resonated in every cell of my body. I became transfixed, the energy was so great. After the talk I went to him and prostrated at his feet. He lifted me up and smiled. I felt love I had never before experienced. I knew then that God, Truth and Mercy were there for everyone. We need only to make the effort, to want it with all our heart.

EDDIE

In essence the journey to wholeness is a pathless path, as it is integral to our every moment. It is an honest, grounded and heartfelt commitment to understanding the nature of existence, the light within the darkness. It is the way home to a place we have never left, for we are uncovering who we already are. A peeling away of the layers that have accumulated so we see the jewel within. It is the journey from here to now, the merging into this timeless moment. In discovering our healing we are discovering ourselves, our beingness, that which is always the same and that which has always been there.

In 1974 I went to visit Sri Nisargadatta in Bombay. I had been ordained a Buddhist monk for four years at that time. He asked me what I had got from those years of simplicity, intensive meditation, monasticism and solitude. I told him absolutely nothing, nothing whatsoever. Nothing had changed at all. How could it? I recall that I broke out into a big smile. He also smiled. Then he got up from his seat and walked over to me, gave me a big hug, and went back to his seat.

CHRISTOPHER TITMUSS

PRACTICE – Walking Our Path

This is a creative visualization that can be done lying down or sitting in a chair. Either way, make sure you are wearing loose, comfortable clothes, that you will be warm enough (use a light blanket if necessary), and that you have a notepad and pen in case you want to write down your feelings or any images that arise. You may find you do not want to do the whole practice in one session, but prefer to do different parts at separate times. This is fine. Take as much time to go through this as you need.

Take a deep breath and let it out slowly through your mouth. Feel yourself beginning to relax and let go of any tension. For a few minutes, focus on your breath as it enters and leaves your body. Just watch the flow of your breath. Become one with that breath. As you do so, feel yourself becoming quieter inside, more at ease and peaceful.

Now bring your attention to the area of your heart. Breathe into your heart, relaxing there for a few minutes. Silently say to yourself, 'I will stay in my heart throughout this practice.'

When you feel relaxed and ready, bring into your heart an image of yourself as a baby. Recognize your parents and other people in your life at that time, and see them as they were then. As you do this keep breathing into your heart. Visualize in your heart the people who were with you in your early years. Stay with this image as long as you want.

Now slowly watch yourself grow. Becoming a child, learning how to walk, how to talk, how to feed yourself, how to play. Connect with yourself as a young child. At the same time recognize all the factors and events that were taking place in your life during those early, formative years. See the people who were with you at that time. See the effect they may have had on you. Just observe. Do not judge or resist. Keep breathing. Take as long as you like.

Now watch yourself as you begin to go to school. Visualize the next few years as you learn how to interact, to write and read, to explore the mental realms. See the people and events in your life then. Can you see any connection between how you are now and what happened to you during these first years of your life? Be aware of what was taking place in your life at this time, at home and with your family. See them, acknowledge them, recognize how they may have affected you. Keep breathing into your heart. Take as much time over this as you need, going through your life year by year.

Now bring into your heart an image of yourself becoming a teenager, dealing with teenage difficulties, with coming maturity. See the events taking place in your life, and the effect that the changing world around you has on your feelings. Visualize the people who were with you, your family and friends. Be aware of your life evolving, of how those things that happened to you in your childhood may now be affecting you as a teenager. See the connections between how you are and all the things that have happened to you. Keep breathing, soft belly.

Slowly watch yourself getting older, moving through your teen years. Observe how you cope, what you do, what happens to you, who you meet. Begin to see a flow taking place, how you are moving from one situation or feeling to another. As you observe, be aware of how each event leads to the next one.

Now bring into your heart an image of yourself entering your early twenties and becoming an adult. Visualize what happened for you. See how you coped with the different things that occurred, what your reactions were. Finishing school, leaving home, making a life for yourself. Simply observe without judgement. Breathe into your heart. Visualize the events that occurred and the people who were with you then. Watch how decisions you made were based on your previous experiences. See how the people you met influenced you. Keep breathing and watching.

In your own time, follow your life on from this point, through your adult years. As you do so, watch the effect from the past and how it influences you. See the thread that connects each relationship, each event, each situation, each feeling. How one leads to another. If painful images arise, know that this is not who you are now. Simply breathe into them and see beyond them, into the learning and growing and into the present. The painful parts of your life are there to help you understand yourself more deeply, to strengthen your wisdom.

As you do this practice, you will become aware of the path you are on. Sink into this path, feel how it has always been there, beneath your feet, even during the times you were not aware of it. See how where you have come from has led to you being here now. Feel the solidity and ground of the path. It is your journey. As each piece of your past fits into place, so your way forward becomes clearer. This is your journey to healing, to wholeness.

Now bring yourself into the present moment and create an awareness of your next step forward. If you need to, ask your inner self what you should do. Take your time. Listen quietly for the answer within and make a commitment to following what you are told.

Slowly become aware of the room around you, of your present self in the world, and how your path *is* your way ahead.

10

CLEAR MIND, OPEN HEART

There is a light that shines beyond all things on earth,
beyond us all, beyond the heavens,
beyond the highest, the very highest heavens.
This is the light that shines in our heart.
CHANDOGYA UPANISHAD (111, 13:7)

When I called to tell my lover of six years that I had tested positive
for the AIDS virus (HIV), the only words I can recall from the
other end of the telephone were, 'How could you do this to me?' and
despite repeated attempts to keep communicating, those were the
last words he chose to leave me with. I was devastated, frantic,
confused and angry. There was also a woman I was romantically
involved with and I had to share the test results with her. She
responded to me with love and compassion, with hope and not fear,
and, to my astonishment, said she would help me through what-
ever lay ahead. Seven years later we have built a home and
marriage together, I remain healthy and she remains HIV nega-
tive. It was her selfless commitment that pulled me from despair
and began to open my heart.

Living with HIV and trying to gain control over it is an
example of the battle I place myself in, getting angry and losing
internal control. My disease may have more to do with my
'dis-ease' when I'm not in control, and with the resultant anger,

than I like to admit. The anger adds more fuel to my disease, robbing my peace and destabilizing my immune system, as well as inflicting disharmony on those around me.

Loving and accepting myself with HIV is the lesson I am learning from my partner. The gentle, reflective and loving approach, versus the 'win the battle' approach, is the gift of her compassion. The bumper sticker that should be tattooed on me is, 'Peace Begins With Me'! Healing comes from inner peace; peace begins with acceptance; acceptance stems from love; love's flower is compassion. I know if I grow these things in my garden, healing will flower and then I can share that in the world I influence. What a gloriously fragrant bouquet – an open heart – what a gift!

T.E.

Seven years ago I was given a rare opportunity. At the time I was a single parent with two children, aged thirteen and ten years, and not looking for Mr Right. But I fell in love and our friendship naturally developed as the magic between us grew. Six months into the relationship he tested HIV positive. I was shocked but not horrified. We watched a friend die of AIDS; both of us were scared. He wanted me to leave him but I couldn't. I knew deep inside that I loved him and that what he needed most in his life was love. We went to Europe for three months, thinking it might be his last vacation.

Now, seven years later, we travel as often as possible and have a great passion for life. We stay informed and educated with the latest information, keep in touch with a circle of HIV positive friends and support groups, but we do not absorb ourselves in the fear of what might happen. I get tested frequently, but, much to everyone's amazement, I remain negative. The process of opening the heart allows new, untouched energy to come forth. In my moments of fear, I think of the pain and suffering that could and does occur. But life is so precious and the moment is gone before we even notice. We cannot exclude fear and suffering from our lives, but we can include love, acceptance and all the goodness that life gives us. The transformation that has taken me from my selfishness into a full commitment to life has shown me compassion, understanding, trust, and to respect the love that is in my heart.

J.E.

As conflicts and crises continually arise to face us, it is vital that we find our healing and open our hearts to others. To live with an open heart is to live with compassion and mercy, embracing our humanness and vulnerability. It is to be courageous in a time of great insecurity. Our lives are like leaves in the wind – there are no guarantees. Yet we can each make a difference. Magic happens when fear is transformed into love, isolation into oneness.

To live with an open heart is to live in a simpler and yet more meaningful way, where we mature into being truly human. When we open our eyes we see beyond our petty differences and personal wants. It is the recognition that we are already free and awake and in love. The truth of ourself is closer than we can imagine, for it is who we already are beneath our searching. What ecstasy there is when we leap from the known into the unknown and find that we have come home! In *Healing into Life and Death*, Stephen Levine writes:

> If healing is, as it seems, the integration of body and mind into the heart, then our only direction has always been healing. . . . Healing is what happens when we come to our edge, to the unexplored territory of mind and body, and take a single step into the unknown, the space in which all growth occurs. . . . Healing occurs not in the tiny thoughts of who we think we are and what we know, but in the vast undefinable spaciousness of being – of what we essentially are – not whom we imagined we shall become.

All of the ancient teachings that have been passed down to us speak of liberation, freedom from suffering, and great awakening. Sri Aurobindo said that to realize this liberation, Nirvana, is not difficult, for it is realizing our essential nature. The challenge lies in bringing this realization into the world. To live with an open heart is to respond to this challenge. It asks of us that we open our arms with compassion, that we learn to bear insult and injury – even to turn the other cheek. When we open to the love in our hearts, then we can embrace the ignorance in the world as a part of our own being.

This is the most rewarding of all challenges as we experience the deepest joy and equanimity. Living in this way is to take down the barriers of separation and to delight in the diversity. It is the purpose, the magic, the healing we took birth for. Jesus spoke of the open heart when he said: 'The Kingdom of Heaven is within.' It is right here and now, in this very moment, accessible to us all.

Now it is time to let my actions come from the knowing that I do not need to act to be worthy of love; for I am already loved. Opening the heart is the healing of the pain of separation; warm, loving energy seals the wound that festers with hate and anger, bitterness and regret. As healing takes place it becomes clearer that the more we go into the heart and are present in the place of love, all our actions become like the rose sending out its fragrance: natural, unforced, simply there because we are alive and it is our nature to love.

HELEN HUMPHRIES

FINDING THE LOVE WITHIN

When we talk about ourselves we usually point to the centre of our chest, to the area of our heart, saying, 'This is me.' We don't point to our head, or to our stomach; we point to our heart. In this area is all the love and the grief, all the compassion and the mercy. It is where our healing lies. In the Eastern teachings this area is known as the heart centre; in opening the heart we awaken to our True Self. An open heart is tender, loving and compassionate. It is an expression of our innermost being, the source of who we really are.

As our heart opens, our mind becomes clear. We see beyond the limitations: how the content is the weightiness – all the labels and identities and roles – while the essence is our lightness. The content is like looking into a mirror and not being able to see through it, seeing only how the dust lies as a heaviness over the lightness of the reflection. It stops us from seeing our true image. Step by step we see the difference

203

between that which is real and meaningful and that which keeps us bound to the meaningless. By paying attention and being open-hearted we connect with the truth. For truth is beautiful, vibrant, like after a rain shower when the sky is full of light, shining and fresh.

There is a basic goodness and sanity within us all that is shown through the open heart. That which can hold and care for another human being, that which can tenderly soothe and embrace another's pain, as if it were our own. It is the realization of this basic goodness and our inherent interdependence that allows us to live fearlessly. We don't need to be enemies, most especially to ourselves. Or to war against each other. But unless the war within ceases, how can the war outside cease? The following stories are examples of how the love within us can heal our wounds and stop the war.

With so many disappointments in my life there was a time when I wasn't quite sure about anything. I had had spiritual experiences but it was early on and I didn't know if they were real or if I was just hallucinating. Doubt would creep into my mind. Every time I tried to be rational, to think things out, I would come up with numerous contradictions that would stimulate fear and resistance. 'What if . . .' became a part of my vocabulary. Immersed in mental dialogue, I questioned my motives, challenging myself until I couldn't make any decisions. I became locked into indecision.

There was a very painful time when I was completely lost in my mind. I was even afraid of the dark so I couldn't go out at night. It seemed like I was in a cocoon of fear. This was my dark night of the soul. Everything appeared impossible, overwhelming. It wasn't easy to get through each day. I was even afraid to answer the telephone, wondering if I could carry on an intelligent conversation! Not knowing what else to do, I prayed for help. I knew I had no choice. From the depths of my being I somehow knew I had to bring my attention to my heart. When I did this my mind would rest. The more I was consciously aware of my heart, the more I was able to bring love into my everyday activities. It worked – in fact it was miraculous! As I focused on the love in the heart, so my mind relaxed and released the fear. I let myself completely sink into my heart. It opened like a flower in the sun.

EDDIE

In 1992 I was diagnosed with cancer and came very close to my own mortality. There were a number of things that stopped me from dying, apart from the skill of the doctors and alternative practitioners that I saw. The principal amongst these was the healing power of love. After going through various stages of fear and disgust after my diagnosis, I finally let love enter into me. I now accept that my existence may last anything between six minutes and sixty years. Each moment has become infinitely more precious in the renewed understanding that whenever I do make the transition it will not be from a place of struggle to one of punishment and judgement, but rather from a place of learning how to love to one where I will be able to practise love fully.

JUSTIN CARSON

I had experienced an emotionally destroying relationship. During the months afterwards, I was immersed in pain and tears. My heart felt wrenched in two, as if I was physically torn open. I would meditate each day, focusing my breath in my heart, longing for relief from the pain. One morning, as I was meditating, I suddenly felt as if my energy was being drawn all the way to the left, pulled all the way into the far, far distance. And there I found, in an empty grey, formless space, a creature, not even human but somehow primordial. It was alone, abandoned, in a barren landscape, misty and bleak. The creature was extreme, pure, total abandonment. And I knew it was me, that part of me that had been so completely abandoned deep inside. And I knew I had to lift it into my arms and slowly I brought it back with me into the present.

But just as I came back into myself it was as if my energy was then pulled away off to the right, all the way to the right. I was being pulled into this soft, warm and luminous space. Standing there was this beautiful figure, bathed in shimmering light. It was the mother. The eternal mother. The only mother. I had an incredible feeling of being nourished and loved by this being. Yet I realized this was me too. And that I had to bring her with me into

205

the present. And she came and the three of us started dancing
together, holding each other. The mother embracing the
abandoned child, the child being nurtured and cared for. And it
was all me. I was both the abandoned child and the loving parent.
I was both the pain and the healing. The love within holding me,
embracing me, healing me.

DEBBIE

OPENING THE HEART OF COMPASSION

The opening of the heart has many different forms of
expression. Moments that lift us to great heights or wrench us
down and tear us apart. There can be an initial wonderment
and ecstasy, only to be followed by fear and panic; a great
sorrow or grief, and then a gentle joyfulness. For in the
tenderness of opening we also experience the sadness and fear
of letting go and of entering into the unknown.

That which arises is not to be dismissed; the pain of the
world fills our being and tears flow freely, we long to hold and
comfort and soothe those who are hurting. It is a natural
movement, an opening that cannot be hurried or forced. An
accepting of the pain into the bountifulness of love. An
acceptance of the love into our whole being.

Neem Karoli Baba said, 'Don't throw anyone out of your
heart.' Not to exclude or dismiss anyone, not to label as
unimportant or unworthy. Not to fall into the trap of
separation, but to stay with the knowledge that we are all equal,
we are all here together, that we are all equally worthy of love.
That each experience can touch us and open our heart
further.

During Holy Week in 1992, Tetsugen Glassman Sensei,
Abbot of the Zen Community of New York, led a retreat on the
streets of the city. The participants ate in soup kitchens, slept
in the streets, did meditation in 'crack park' and spent most of
their time looking for places to relieve themselves. One of the
participants, Rick Fields, said:

The street stripped away all expectations. It left us nowhere to hide. It left us nowhere to rest the body, and it left us nowhere for the mind to abide. It eased, if only for a few days, the line between us and them. Such exposure can be both devastating and enlightening. There is so much suffering and love out there, in here. It's enough to break your heart right open.

The pain of the heart is our responding to the pain of the suffering of humankind. We hurt each other so blindly, so carelessly. We destroy each other and our world with no thought of the future. It is easy to feel hopeless – to want to walk away from it all. The joy of the heart is the experience of love that fills our every cell, that pulsates throughout our being, that uplifts us into a compassionate embrace with all life. We are tested and challenged in every moment: every time we are tempted to close our heart and turn away, but instead we choose to stay open and loving.

> *I feel with people. If someone is bereaved, I cry with them. I can see the burnt out bodies in Bosnia and feel the despair of the way we are as human beings. I stay with the pain and let it touch me. I talk and share this despair so it does not become trapped inside; I want to explore my feelings. Doing this helps me live with it. I have a vision of what humanity could be, all of us together celebrating each other's perspective of God. We could actually live like this. Respecting each other. The dance of the Hindu, the stillness of the Buddhist monk, the passion of the Muslim, the naked emotion of the Jew, the devotion of the Christian – each a different quality yet together making a whole.*
>
> MALCOLM STERN

In a sermon to the governing board of the US National Council of Churches, Archbishop Desmond Tutu pleaded, 'Please make it fashionable to be compassionate.' In its most altruistic sense, compassion is a heartfelt longing of love and mercy that all beings be free from suffering, a deeply motivating energy that fills our being. It is the objective expression of unconditional love, where we are moved to act through the depth of our understanding and empathy. In recognizing our essential interconnectedness we cannot separate another's pain from ourselves. As the controversial Trappist monk Thomas Merton says, 'Compassion is the keen awareness of the interdependence of all living things which are all involved and are all a part of one another.'

We are constantly confronted with situations that draw on this: seeing homeless people on the street, watching Bosnians or Serbs or Ethiopians trying to survive, the hatred of racial or religious prejudice, the pain of abuse and violence, and the selfishness of greed. There is no end to the myriad ways in which we can practise compassion, for there is no end to the causes of suffering. Albert Einstein said,

> A human being is a part of the whole called by us the universe, a part limited in time and space. He experiences himself, his thoughts and feelings as something separated from the rest, a kind of optical delusion of his consciousness. This delusion is a kind of prison for us, restricting us to our personal desires and to affection for a few persons nearest to us. Our task must be to free ourselves of this prison by widening our circle of compassion to embrace all living creatures and the whole of nature in its beauty.

Yet what does it take to be a compassionate person, to have the 'compassion to embrace all living creatures'? The amount of suffering is enormous and we may feel powerless in the face of it. We cannot all go to Africa to feed the starving, nor create homes for all the homeless. How do we decide where we can be of most help? How do we say no to some and yes to others?

To be compassionate, it seems we also need the ability to discern and discriminate, to see where our action can be of real help and value, or where it may simply be supporting an already unhealthy situation. This second stance is known as idiot compassion. True compassion is inherently skilful as it brings release from suffering; idiot compassion is not skilful and therefore may create more suffering.

208

In Tibetan Buddhism there is a wonderful image of Manjushri, the Buddha of Wisdom, who holds in his hand a flaming sword – the sword of wisdom. This sword is used to cut through ignorance and delusion, through that which limits our awakening. But if we use the sword on its own, without compassion, the cut can hurt and bleed. So beside Manjushri there is the image of Avalokiteshvara, the Buddha of Compassion, who has eleven heads and a thousand arms with an eye in each palm, for compassion sees and reaches in all directions.

Compassion without wisdom can become idiot compassion as there is the desire to give but there is not the means to discern what is needed. Bringing wisdom and compassion together means that when we use the sword of wisdom the cut will not bleed, for it is done with love. It also means we see more clearly where and how compassionate action is needed. In *Seeking the Heart of Wisdom*, J. Goldstein and J. Kornfield speak of how:

> When we realise in our own experience that happiness comes not from reaching out but from letting go, not from seeking pleasurable experience but from opening in the moment to what is true, this transformation of understanding then frees the energy of compassion within us. Our minds are no longer bound in pushing away pain or holding on to pleasure. Compassion becomes the natural response of an open heart.

Compassion is usually associated with gentle, non-judgemental awareness of the suffering of others. But the Tibetan images suggest another aspect – a cutting through the delusion and ignorance. For instance, a friend comes to you with their problems. You listen and offer support and advice. The next time you see this person they are still moaning about the same thing. However, you decide not to say anything as you do not wish to appear unsympathetic or uncaring. You keep listening and offering your help, but it goes nowhere. Each time you see this person the same thing happens. Eventually you have to tell them how they are limiting their healing. Being compassionate may hurt a little but it also illuminates, whereas idiot compassion may appear to be supportive but does not necessarily help release the suffering.

The compassionate act is not always easy to define; it requires creativity and presence in each moment. Maintaining peace within ourselves is an act of compassion, even if it means saying no to others at certain times and thus appearing as if we lack compassion. Always saying yes and helping whenever we are asked or putting other's needs ahead of our own often means we are saying no to ourselves. Soon we lose our peace and our giving becomes resentful – we feel like a martyr, or we get exhausted and stop being able to give at all.

In any healthy relationship there has to be a balance between our own needs and those of others. When we say yes to ourselves we are being our own friend. When we are peaceful we can give far more. Many people ask how can they be at peace when there are people starving in Africa or suffering elsewhere. But suffering more because of the pain in the world does not help those who are already suffering. As each of us connects with our own peace, then there is one less person in pain. When we are true to ourselves and our own needs, we can be of far greater benefit to the whole. As the Buddhist teacher Tai Situ Rinpoche says in *The Way Ahead:*

> Do not make the mistake of thinking you are a powerless individual in a vast world. Know that you are armed with three great powers. You have the power of the body (the source of all action), the power of speech (the source of all expression), and the power of the mind (the source of all thought). Use them wisely and with great compassion.

AWAKENING TO OUR TRUE SELF

When we wake up from having a dream during the night we might say, 'Oh, that was a dream!' All that had seemed so real in the dream is suddenly seen for what it is, for being insubstantial and unreal. We may feel elated or relieved, depending on the nature of the dream. But we are now awake, so the dream soon becomes unimportant and fades from our memory.

When we wake up from our everyday state to the higher state of liberation, to the awakened state, the world as we know it appears like a dream. We are in a place where there are no boundaries. We see the interplay of dramas that keep people separated and isolated from each other, bound by fear, and we see it as if it were a dream.

In May of 1991 I was in Miami Airport waiting to catch a plane. It was early morning so I stopped for coffee and a roll. A nice middle-aged black lady whose name tag said 'Annie' was fussing around the cafeteria and helped me find milk for my coffee. Being a bit sleep-deprived, I put too much in my cup. Annie suggested more coffee to rebalance the milk. I said to her, 'I just need to wake up.' 'That's what life is all about, isn't it?' she said, 'Waking up.' I made some kind of dopey comment and found a table to sit at. Then 'Boing!' The coin dropped, the energy moved and for the hundredth time the teachings came from an unlooked-for source.

NANCY FORD KOHNE

The path to an open heart, to the truth that is ever present, is about un-knowing, or un-doing. We have been taught so much and have learnt so many different things that we have become amazing storehouses of information. But when we release ourselves from the judgements, prejudices, dogmas and intellectual rationalities we discover something entirely different from what we ever knew before. As Lao Tzu said, 'He who knows much about others may be learned, but he who understands himself is more intelligent. He who controls others may be powerful, but he who has mastered himself is mightier still.'

The undoing, unknowing and unlearning is about becoming empty and seeing the fullness, the vastness beyond our limited self. It is knowing more than we ever knew because the screen of illusion has been removed. This is the clear mind. It is an intuitive, inner knowing. Like knowing that the stars will be out at night or that the sun is there even on a cloudy day. Stephen Levine says in *Healing into Life and Death:* 'The path of

211

healing is . . . a coming home, a return of the living moment. But because there is so much more to us than just mind/body, because our original nature is without boundary, its edgelessness cannot be described. It can only be participated in.'

Each of us has our own sense of that which is beyond our everyday reality: that which can be held but is beyond holding, can be touched but is beyond touching, can be tasted but is beyond tasting, can be smelt but is beyond smelling, can be heard but is beyond hearing, is everywhere and in all things and yet is to be found nowhere. A sense of a non-conceptual creator or an energy that is beyond our limited awareness. In this context, when we speak of God we mean the awakened mind, all-pervading pure consciousness, omnipresent and omnipotent. The force that is the infinite potential within each one of us. The ocean of consciousness of which each of us is a part.

I was sitting quietly in our living room when suddenly there was a great presence, a wonderful feeling of peace. I had been raised to believe that God is invisible. Yet in that moment I suddenly realized what invisible really meant: that it is visible within, is in-visible. To see within, to be within the vision. It was as if I suddenly became more alive – my mind became so clear I felt I dissolved into a blissful ocean of consciousness, a drop merging into the ocean and then becoming a drop again. There was an unexplainable sense of joy and bliss and the whole room was bright. Everything at that moment was understood! God is visible within!

EDDIE

That invisible force is always there – the supreme awareness that is closer to us than we are to ourselves. When the little self that we call 'me' merges with the greater 'I', then the invisible becomes visible. How wonderful, how inspiring and uplifting! As we peel away the veils of ignorance, the layers of illusion and breathe very deeply into our hearts, then we see that all our searching was to discover our own selves. We awaken to the joy and happiness that is who we are and always have been. As we open our hearts, the clarity of peace, the luminous mind, emerges.

On my third evening in Cyprus I was sitting vacantly gazing over the sea, near the port of Limassol, when the turning point of my life occurred. A strange feeling crept upon me, like the sensation of a hand caressing the back of my neck and tingling its way up over the top of my head. My skin went all goose-pimply. I had the impression of another 'ghostly' brain being pressed into mine, and my body seemed to dissolve.

Suddenly my consciousness was no longer limited to the body and expanded rapidly across the earth and the ocean and into space. Instantaneously I was aware of being everywhere in the universe at the same time. The normal functioning of mind and intellect was completely bypassed by this experience, but suddenly I understood there was an Omnipresent Consciousness underlying the whole universe. And when my own notion of myself dissolved like salt in the ocean, I became That, I was none other than That – the Omnipresence. When I found myself back in the body again, I realized with awe that we were all That in the guise of human beings. Life was never to be the same again.

MUZ MURRAY

One morning I was practising meditation – Loving Kindness meditation – when I heard the post van drive up. Footsteps on the gravel sounded like they were coming straight to me, and then I felt a huge key rattle in the lock of my heart. As it did I became suffused with love from head to toe. I laughed happily at the absurdity and glory of it all!

KARUNA KING

To enter the Kingdom of Heaven it is said that we need to be like a child. Not childish but childlike. A child does not hold on to things for too long. As we get older we hold on to our toys and take life more seriously – sometimes too seriously! Why should we no longer think we are not a child? There is a humorous saying: 'Why do angels fly? Because they take themselves lightly!' There is nothing we can hold on to. This is so liberating! We came into this world with nothing and we can take nothing with us when we leave. When we fully experience this we can dance, we can play, we can enjoy this life!

I was walking in Battersea Park, by the Peace Pagoda, when it suddenly struck me how God had created humankind in the image of God in order to have playmates. The thought of this made me laugh out loud! It seemed so ironic. For the difficulty is that humankind forgot about this and started playing with each other. If only we could see and play with the God in each other.

EDDIE

Love is the essence of all existence. It is the sustaining force of the universe, the invincible, invisible hand that supports the earth and the stars and the moon and the sun. It is the sound of life, the beat of our hearts, the rain on our faces. It is the power and glory, the mystery and magic in every moment. Love is the genius of creation that is an unending source of giving, like a mother to a newborn baby, or the fruit that falls from a tree, or the air that enables us to breathe. Love is the open heart. It is our healing. It is through love that the mind discovers its innate wisdom. The brilliance beyond the intellect, the peace beyond understanding, the clarity that needs no explanation. With a clear mind and an open heart may we live in this world with peace.

PRACTICE – The Development of Loving-Kindness

This meditation practice helps us develop a deeper experience of open heart and loving-kindness. Either read this practice on to a tape, ask a friend to read it to you, or there is a tape available by the authors. Start by finding a comfortable sitting position, whether cross-legged on the floor or sitting in a chair (with the feet flat on the floor), the spine upright and the eyes closed. Hands are resting in the lap. Take a deep breath and relax.

In this meditation you discover that to develop

214

unconditional love you have to start by loving yourself, just as you are, fully and unconditionally. This is not always easy, but it is essential. By looking at and accepting all that which is stopping you from loving yourself, you develop true unconditional love for all others.

Start by focusing on your breathing for a few minutes. Gently watching the in and out breath, the flow of the breath, becoming one with this flow.

Now bring your attention to the area of your heart; just sink into the heart. Breathe into the heart. Then bring into your heart an image of yourself, just as you are now. Hold yourself in your own heart, as a mother would hold a child: gently, compassionately. Then silently repeat to yourself, 'May I be well, may I be happy, may I be free.' Keep repeating these words in your heart.

As you do this, acknowledge any opposing thoughts that might arise: reasons why you should not be happy, or not be well, feelings of guilt or shame and of not being worthy, or your inability to receive love. Acknowledge these and let them go. Continue doing this and repeating, 'May I be well, may I be happy, may I be free,' for the next few minutes, holding yourself gently and lovingly.

Now direct your loving-kindness and compassion towards a near and dear friend. Choose someone who does not stimulate parental or romantic feelings in you, so as to allow true unconditional love to develop. Bring this person into your heart, holding them with your loving-kindness and compassion, and silently repeating, 'May they be well, may they be happy, may they be free.'

Acknowledge any feelings of competition or jealousy that may arise and let these feelings go. Continue this for a few minutes, allowing your love for this person to fill your entire being.

Now direct your loving-kindness and compassion towards a neutral person, someone for whom you have neither positive nor negative feelings. You may not even know his or her name, for when we know someone we immediately have a specific feeling about them. So it may be just someone who works in a store, or delivers the post, someone whose face you remember. Find this neutral person and bring them into your heart and let unconditional love flow towards them. Repeat in your heart, 'May they be well, may they be happy, may they be free.'

You are feeling a love for the unknown. And you begin to realize that it is not the personality that you are loving, for in this case you do not even know the personality. Rather, it is the essence of being human, the very beingness that we all share. This is what you are loving. And it is in you as much as it is in every other person. Feel your love expanding towards even those who are unknown to you. This may seem odd or difficult at first, but keep going for a few minutes.

Now direct your loving-kindness and compassion towards one with whom you are experiencing conflict, where there is some form of negative communication. This may be a relative, friend or colleague – anyone with whom all is not right. Bring this person into your heart and begin to expand your loving-kindness and compassion even to them. Let your acceptance and love flow towards them. 'May they be well, may they be happy, may they be free.'

Remember that pain, and hurt, and anger are born out of forgetfulness – out of the forgetfulness of our essential interdependency – and you can forgive this. In forgiving others, you are also forgiving yourself. Holding this person in your heart, you expand your forgiveness, love and compassion. Feel your heart opening towards this person, for there is no real separation between you.

Now, hold these four people in your heart: yourself, your dear friend, the neutral person and the one you are in conflict with, and feel such love and compassion towards all four equally that if you were asked to choose one in preference over the others, you would not be able to do so. Let your love flow towards all four, unconditionally.

From these four you now begin to expand your loving-kindness towards all other beings. Your love radiates outwards, like the ripples on a pond, reaching out towards all beings in all directions. The love in your heart expands to all beings, everywhere. 'May all beings be well, may all beings be happy, may all beings be free. May all beings be at peace and may I be at peace with all beings.'

Feel your love suffusing throughout your entire being. Feel the warmth of this love. As you gently come out of this meditation, feel that love filling you with joy and have a big smile on your lips! Thank you.

INDEX

ABOUT THE AUTHORS

Eddie Shapiro was born in New York in 1942. As a teenager he won the New York City dance championships. In 1968, after meeting some of the outstanding spiritual teachers of the time, he was invited to train in India. There he became a monk and laid the foundation for the work to which he and his wife, the well-known author Debbie Shapiro, have dedicated their lives.

Debbie was born near London in 1953 to a family of Quaker background. She trained for many years in bodymind therapy, traditional Eastern meditation and philosophy, in both London and America. Together they have received personal teachings and transmission from the Dalai Lama, Tai Situ Rinpoche and prominent Indian yogis such as Paramhamsa Satyananda and Swami Satchidananda.

The Shapiros are inspired workshop leaders who often give presentations at international conferences, and have featured on television, radio and in magazines worldwide. They are the American representatives to the Holy Isle Project. They have recently moved from Boulder, Colorado, USA where Eddie was a freestyle skier, to Devon, England, where they have established the Maitri Retreat Centre (Maitri means compassionate friendship) for those interested in personal growth, healing and self-realization.

Eddie and Debbie Shapiro have been recognized by their peers for making a major contribution to the upliftment of individual and social consciousness. Dr Bernie Siegel, author of million bestseller *Love Medicine and Miracles*, says, 'Eddie and Debbie Shapiro are two warm, capable and caring individuals. Their work makes our planet a safer and more loving place to live.' Dr Lex Hixon, author of *Great Swan* and *Mother of the Buddhas*, says, 'The wonderful Shapiros are a conduit of joy and spiritual energy that heals hearts on their subtle levels. They bypass the ordinary mental patterns of our culture, yet present themselves in a relaxed, natural manner, totally in terms of modern culture.'

BOOKS BY THE CROSSING PRESS

Conscious Marriage:
From Chemistry to Communication
By John C. Lucas, Ph.D.

In this blueprint for building a successful relationship, John C. Lucas charts the stages of our relationships and shows us what we need to make them grow into joyous, fulfilled marriages. He teaches us how to identify and solve problems, how to build a healthy foundation, and how to land on our feet when we fall in love.

$14.95 • Paper • 0-89594-915-6

Pocket Guide To Meditation
By Alan L. Pritz

This book focuses on meditation as part of spiritual practice, as a universal tool to forge a deeper connection with spirit. In Alan Pritz's words, "Meditation simply delivers one of the most purely profound experiences of life, joy."

$6.95 • Paper • 0-89594-886-9

Pocket Guide To Visualization
By Helen Graham

Visualization is imagining; producing mental images that come to mind as pictures we can see. These pictures can help you relax, assess and manage stress, improve self-awareness, control your life, alleviate disease, manage pain and find your Higher Self.

$6.95 • Paper • 0-89594-885-0

Chakras and Their Archetypes:
Uniting Energy Awareness and Spiritual Growth
By Ambika Wauters

Linking classic archetypes to the seven chakras in the human energy system can reveal unconscious ways of behaving. Wauters helps us understand where our energy is blocked, which attitudes or emotional issues are responsible, and how to then transcend our limitations.

$16.95 • Paper • 0-89594-891-5

BOOKS BY THE CROSSING PRESS

The Language of Dreams

By Patricia Telesco

Patricia Telesco outlines a creative, interactive approach to understanding the dream symbols of our inner life. Interpretations of more than 800 dream symbols incorporate multi-cultural elements with psychological, religious, folk, and historical meanings.

$16.95 • Paper • 0-89594-836-2

The Sevenfold Journey:
Reclaiming Mind, Body & Spirit Through the Chakras

By Anodea Judith and Selene Vega

Combining yoga, movement, psychotherapy, and ritual, the authors weave ancient and modern wisdom into a powerful tapestry of techniques for facilitating personal growth and healing.

$18.95 • Paper • 0-89594-574-6

Wishing Well:
Empowering Your Hopes and Dreams

By Patricia Telesco

Blending folklore, magic, and creative visualization, author Patricia Telesco explains how reclaiming the practice of Wishcraft can create our reality exactly as we wish it to be.

$14.95 • Paper • 0-89594-870-2

Your Body Speaks Your Mind:
How Your thoughts and Emotions Affect Your Health

By Debbie Shapiro

Debbie Shapiro examines the intimate connection between the mind and body revealing insights into how our unresolved thoughts and feelings affect our health and manifest as illness in specific parts of the body.

$14.95 • Paper • 0-89594-893-1

Books by The Crossing Press

**Pocket Guide to
Acupressure Points
for Women**
By Cathryn Bauer
$6.95 • ISBN 0-89594-879-6

**Pocket Guide to
Aromatherapy**
By Kathi Keville
$6.95 • ISBN 0-89594-815-X

**Pocket Guide to
Astrology**
By Alan Oken
$6.95 • ISBN 0-89594-820-6

**Pocket Guide to
Ayurvedic Healing**
By Candis Cantin Packard
$6.95 • ISBN 0-89594-764-1

**Pocket Guide to Bach
Flower Essences**
By Rachelle Hasnas
$6.95 • ISBN 0-89594-865-6

**Pocket Guide to
Celtic Spirituality**
By Sirona Knight
$6.95 • ISBN 0-89594-907-5

**Pocket Guide to
Fortunetelling**
By Scott Cunningham
$6.95 • ISBN 0-89594-875-3

**Pocket Guide to
Good Food**
By Margaret M. Wittenberg
$6.95 • ISBN 0-89594-747-1

**Pocket Guide to
Hatha Yoga**
By Michele Picozzi
$6.95 • ISBN 0-89594-911-3

**Pocket Herbal
Reference Guide**
By Debra St. Claire
$6.95 • ISBN 0-89594-568-1

**Pocket Guide to
Macrobiotics**
By Carl Ferré
$6.95 • ISBN 0-89594-848-6

**Pocket Guide to
Midwifery Care**
By Aviva Jill Romm
$6.95 • ISBN 0-89594-855-9

BOOKS BY THE CROSSING PRESS

Pocket Guide to Naturopathic Medicine
By Judith Boice
$6.95 • ISBN 0-89594-821-4

Pocket Guide to Numerology
By Alan Oken
$6.95 • ISBN 0-89594-826-5

Pocket Guide to Self Hypnosis
By Adam Burke, Ph.D., M.P.H.
$6.95 • ISBN 0-89594-824-9

Pocket Guide to Shamanism
By Tom Cowan
$6.95 • ISBN 0-89594-845-1

Pocket Guide to the Tarot
By Alan Oken
$6.95 • ISBN 0-89594-822-2

Pocket Guide to The 12 Steps
By Kathleen S.
$6.95 • ISBN 0-89594-864-8

Pocket Guide to Wicca
By Rev. Paul Tuitéan & Estelle Daniels
$6.95 • ISBN 0-89594-904-0

To receive a current catalog from The Crossing Press
please call toll-free, 800-777-1048.
Visit our Web site on the Internet: www. crossingpress.com